FIRESIDE

Other books by Lenny Lipton

(Published by Simon and Schuster)

Independent Filmmaking
The Super 8 Book

*(To be published by The University
of California Press)*

A Study in Depth: Foundations of the
Stereoscopic Cinema

LIPTON ON FILMMAKING

by Lenny Lipton

EDITED BY Chet Roaman

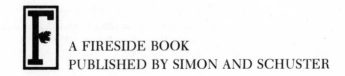

A FIRESIDE BOOK
PUBLISHED BY SIMON AND SCHUSTER

A Fireside Book
Published by Simon and Schuster
A Division of Gulf & Western Corporation
Simon & Schuster Building
Rockefeller Center
1230 Avenue of the Americas
New York, New York 10020

Designed by Irving Perkins
Manufactured in the United States of America

1 2 3 4 5 6 7 8 9 10
1 2 3 4 5 6 7 8 9 10 Pbk.

Library of Congress Cataloging in Publication Data

Lipton, Leonard.
    Lipton on filmmaking.
    1. Cinematography.   I. Roaman, Chet, date.
II. Title.
TR850.L622   778.5   79–215

ISBN 0–671–24427–2
ISBN 0–671–24791–3 Pbk.

"Will Polavision Be the 'Big Mac' of Super 8?" is based on "Instant Movies from Polaroid," previously printed in the Filmcraft column of *Super 8 Filmaker*, Vol. 5, No. 5, July/August 1977, copyright © 1977 by *Super 8 Filmaker*.

"One Step Backward, A Big Step Forward" is based on "How Instant Film Works," previously printed in the Filmcraft column of *Super 8 Filmaker*, Vol. 6, No. 5, July/August 1978, copyright © 1978 by *Super 8 Filmaker*.

"The Truth Behind the XL Camera Boom" is based on "The Truth About XL Cameras," previously printed in the Filmcraft column of *Super 8 Filmaker*, Vol. 5, No. 7, November 1977, copyright © 1977 by *Super 8 Filmaker*.

"Power to Spare" is based on "Super Power Your Camera," previously

For Julie

Acknowledgments

Most of the articles in this book have been collected from columns appearing regularly in the magazine *Super-8 Filmaker* (they're stingy with *m*'s). Others come from *American Cinematographer* and one, "Straight Talk from a Basement Filmmaker," was originally commissioned by *Evergreen Review*. Several pieces, written especially for this book, have not seen print before. All these articles, which were written within the past few years, have been revised and updated to reflect my hopefully maturing opinions and the ever-changing technology of filmmaking. In many cases, they've been so heavily revised, they barely resemble the original. All to the good.

My film work has been almost entirely in the medium of super 8 ("Filming *Le Pink Grapefruit*," a 16mm project, is the exception), and the articles reflect this.

I would like to thank Bruce Anderson, editor of *Super-8 Filmaker*, and Herb Lightman, editor of *American Cinematographer*, for permission to use material which first appeared in their publications. I would also like to thank the many people who supplied me with technical information about their products, but I can't possibly remember everybody who helped, so if I don't list any of you, you must forgive me.

Contents

10   Contents

SECTION 4   Afterimage

SECTION 5   The Shape of Images to Come

Introduction:

Straight Talk
from a Basement Filmmaker

Midnight is a terrible time for looking at films, unless you get out of bed around noon. Now that I "work for myself," to recall a phrase I use at tax time, I sometimes stay in bed all day, but only when I'm feeling really great. In New York, in the early sixties, when I was in my early twenties, I felt myself locked into a nine-to-five existence, and midnight was a terrible time for looking at movies.

But midnight was the only hour you could get to see what are called *underground* or *experimental* films at some screening uptown or downtown. They moved from theater to theater like a permanent floating crap game.

Movies. I love movies, like just about everybody else. I have loved movies even though my earliest movie memory is the witch in Disney's *Snow White*. My mother had to haul me screaming from the theater, I was so terrified. I couldn't have been more than six, at the kiddie show at the Ambassador Theater on Saratoga Avenue in Brooklyn. Out of the theater, into the striped sunlight under the El tracks, and into the afternoon's bus fumes.

Shift the scene from Brooklyn to Manhattan, 20 years later, and make it midnight screenings instead of noontime kiddie shows.

The author (photo by Rod Wyatt).

On one particular midnight, a Saturday night, at the New Yorker Theater, in the company of magician and photographer Charlie Reynolds, I saw part of Stan Brakhage's *Dog Star Man*.

I couldn't believe my eyes. What was this guy trying to do to my eyeballs? This stuff . . . it was . . . well, it looked like junk. The cutting was too rapid, and the colors were weird, and it was silent, and everything was double, sometimes even triple exposed. And what was it about? I hated it.

We talked about the man and his work, and I remember that Charlie spoke about knowing Maya Deren, who had influenced the young Stan Brakhage. But that had been 20 years before. Brakhage had moved light-years away from the roots of Deren's work, like Freud and surrealism. The flow of Brakhage's work was unlike anything I was accustomed to, and I felt there was no form because I did not perceive any. His work ran so counter to my notions of what to expect from a film, that the man and his work pissed me off.

A few weeks later, I was sitting in on a private screening at the Museum of Modern Art (MOMA) when Brakhage's *Prelude to Dog Star Man* was shown. My head opened up. I mean this quite literally. As I watched those crazy and incomprehensible images, my field of vision expanded, and the small rectangle of movie screen in front of me filled the universe as if it were projected clear to the back of my skull.

I "understood" Brakhage's message, his theme, his plot, his characterizations. I knew what it was about. This was a moment of true transcendent insight, purely nonintellectual, and my perception of the world, and of film, like it or not, had been changed.

Although I could not articulate what had happened to me at the time, in today's parlance it's easily put: My mind had been blown. Now I understand what happened. He had no respect for me, or the audience. Brakhage had a lack of respect, and an artist should have respect for the dead—his audience.

Those Old Testament prophets, they were crazy guys. A flash like the one I had just had was all it took to set them on their way. I had seen the light, Moses' burning bush. Did this epiphany set me on my way? Not at once, not that minute. I kept quiet about my flash, then and there at least. I sat in the dark between films while the man who was in charge of MOMA's film thing sat there and grumbled, very much as I had only days before. This complaining sounded obscene to my ears, which were now attached to an enlightened head. But what was the basis of my new-found knowledge? What property of the cinema had Brakhage exploited to have such an effect on me?

My path was changed because of "Breakage," as I sometimes call him, for he had broken my tie with the intellectually based cinema. There is no turning back from such deep knowledge. You do not have to embrace the flash immediately, but to ignore it is to live half dead, responding to gray shadows, unable to make the effort to perceive life's richly colored substance.

The blast of eye-squinting sunlight, *"Snow White"* light, out there on the streets after leaving an afternoon screening made me leave the world of dreams, of epiphany. I had left the dark mansion of the movies. I stepped out of the MOMA screening room, onto the streets of New York, and now I had to deal with survival. I was headed downtown to the editorial offices of *Popular Photography*.

Just weeks before—it was 1964—I had been on the edge of quitting my job at *Popular Photography*, and on the very day of the very edge, I walked into the office of the "maniac-in-chief" with my resignation speech, if not well memorized, then at least well rehearsed. Before I had the words out of my mouth, the editor had offered me the job of editor of the movie section of the magazine. Obviously this man did not know that I loved films and had been making my own 8mm movies for two years. If he had known, I would never have gotten the job.

Up from oblivion, I ran pieces about the Kuchar brothers, Stan VanDerBeek, Jonas Mekas, and the Filmmakers' Cooperative. It was a golden age for the movie section of the magazine, or maybe it was fool's gold, but I began to meet filmmakers like George and Mike Kuchar, Ed Emshwiller, and VanDerBeek. Bob Christgau, now a popular music critic, and I helped run the film screenings at the Eventorium for a year or so, and during that time, I was exposed to a lot of films and works in progress.

The filmmakers were as important to me as their films. Here were people who were devoting their lives to films of personal expression. They were like painters or sculptors or other artists. Who ever heard of filmmakers like these? They weren't making films for Hollywood or Standard Oil; they were making intimate films, deeply felt films which moved me, films that mirrored the longings of the psyche, deep dreams, films about the most god-awful neurotic hangups, or films celebrating life's sunny energy.

Somehow these people, these filmmakers, survived—even, after a fashion, flourished. If the world of filmmaking is a great mansion, these people had found a place in its basement. And I dreamed of becoming one of them, a basement filmmaker, making films at bargain prices.

I was not completely unprepared for what was happening to me in New York. I had been out of school for two or three years and, in 1962, when I left Cornell University, was only vaguely aware of the works of the American avant-garde, in touch primarily through Jonas Mekas's column in the *Village Voice*. The only film by an independent artist I can remember seeing while hiding out in Ithaca was James Broughton's *Looney Tom,* that Chaplinesque satyr dancing through pastoral settings. Until I saw Broughton's film, I had little idea that the motion picture could be a lyrical form.

In the early sixties, Mekas helped to publicize the work of film artists like Gregory Markopoulas, Kenneth Anger, Jack Smith, Ron Rice, Ken Jacobs, Bruce Baillie, Bob Nelson, and others. Mekas's approach to film criticism was refreshing, and I found the words he wrote in those years to be an inspiration. Even among movie critics he was considered a first-class nut. You see, he would say how he felt about a film or a filmmaker, and he was usually hysterically enthusiastic. He knew instinctively that art and life are about feelings, which is a revolutionary thing in a world of mental midgets who have a permanent case of emotional constipation, a logjam preventing any upfront revelation of self.

Through the endurance that can only come with clear vision, Mekas influenced me and, as if this isn't enough, I believe the entire course of the history of film. A person with clear vision is a rare and powerful wonder. The minds of most, as if subject to the influence of the Invisible Shadow, are clouded. A person who can see clearly is a person of power.

Mekas's version of the "film poet" (his term or Cocteau's) was the romantic vision of the starving artist in the lonely garret. This bohemian conception greatly appealed to me, even though I had endured a student diet of peanut butter and boiled potatoes. Mekas wrote one column about Jack Smith, whose infamous film *Flaming Creatures* was setting records for police confiscation. Smith's decadent transvestite orgy seems silly to me, now as then, and by *Green Door* standards, it is mild. But all the same, Smith was filming his vision, which was strongly felt and, by God, somehow lyrical, even if it was daffy.

Mekas described Smith's dire poverty, his eating four-day-old oatmeal and bits of onions, if I remember correctly. I have no desire to mock Smith's misfortune, but somehow this image worked its way into my mind, and in those days, I often thought of Smith in his loft or garret. I thought about his ordeal of oatmeal, and I too dreamed of making films, scraping four-day-old oatmeal out of battered pans, chewing on tough old onions.

Within a few months, I had begun my first 16mm film, *Happy Birthday, Lenny*. It cost very little to make, probably less than $200, and I was able to borrow all the equipment I needed. *Happy Birthday, Lenny*'s first public screening took place at the Flaherty Film Seminar. The reaction was overwhelming; most of the seminarians hated it. One person called the film "vomit." Another said I had no right to make such a film. It's not pornographic or politically radical or scatological, but on that day in August 1965, it was offensive.

The film is simply constructed. The track consists of my mother crying and complaining about the spiritual loss of her son. Her anguished voice is heard while images from my life flow by. Few human beings are shown, and the images are formal. The synchronization of sound and picture is casual, or what I think Jung would call synchronistic, rather than casual. It is a film about the pain of separation, the nature of love, need, and although the term didn't exist then, there's no doubt that it's a film about the generation gap.

Look how far I had come! A few months before, I was complaining about Brakhage's film, and now people were complaining about mine. I was on my way. I had become a filmmaker in the basement of the mansion. My film was not respectable. And why should it have been? Maybe the art which society condemns is like strong medicine which tastes bad, but does you a lot of good in the long run.

One day, a couple of years after my first screening of *Happy Birthday, Lenny*, I lay flat on my back in my yard. Within my house, friends were partying, while there with my head in the grass, I gazed up at blue sky and a few streaks of clouds. I was looking at visions and shapes that formed themselves out of the clouds.

The grain and texture of the sky revealed itself to me, and the world opened up, filling the inside of my skull at first with visions, and then with an engulfing white light which grew from out of the ozone. The experience came as much from within me as it did from a tab of LSD, or from God on high in the sky. As you probably have recognized, the experience sounds like my second viewing of *Prelude to Dog Star Man*. By that time, I had moved to California, had completed five or so short films, and was working on *Show and Tell*, my first film beyond the 10-minute length.

The similarity of my LSD and film experiences has caused a lot of churning in my mind. For years now, I have considered the matter. Usually I give most thought to these things when I'm editing, rather than shooting. Editing is an inward pursuit, an implosive process, not necessarily any more or less intellectual than shooting. For me, though, holding a camera is expansive and explosive, and I'm less given to introspection at this time. So I think about filmmaking more when I'm editing. Although filmmakers train their perception and appreciation of the visceral nature of the medium, using the intellect as much as possible, ultimately what we call intellect is secondary to actual perception and creation.

I ask myself questions like this: What is the deep nature of film? It has occupied so much of my life, and continues to consume my interest, yet I have no answer. I have some tentative thoughts that I can share with you, although a working filmmaker is a pragmatist, operating on a gut level, less interested in theory than in results on the screen.

Physicists claim that objective reality exists within their laboratories, and judges think it lives in their courtrooms, and Walter Cronkite on his evening news. The wise filmmaker knows better. It's easy to be seduced by film's apparent ability to reproduce objective reality. The film image appears to be whole, concrete, and so filled with detail and texture, that this shadowy technological triumph seems to have substance and equal weight with daily life.

But film is a phantom. It does not need to compete directly with the real world of stimuli. The nature of the film experience cries out that film is magic to be harnessed. A few theatrical directors, like Eisenstein and Cocteau, have realized this. The basement filmmaker—the independent or underground filmmaker if you like—realizes that this is a fundamental axiom. After all, during much of the time we spend looking at that seemingly substantial image, we are actually looking at nothing at all. Because of the action of the projector shutter, the screen is frequently empty. Call it a movie, call it a dream, but half the time you're looking at a blank screen.

Some filmmakers, like Tony Conrad and Peter Kubelka, have exploited this aspect of the medium through film of flickering or flashing light, composed along lines of mathematical progressions, using carefully calculated alternations of clear and black frames. Such experiments take film to the heart of its creative energy: the individual frame.

Brakhage has based part of his esthetic, as I understand it, on this discrete "flickering" nature of film, and another part of his esthetic on the closely linked concept of the perception of grain. The motion picture is made up of separate frames, and each frame is made up of grain. The photographic image is built of grain.

In color photography, dye replaces the silver grains of black-and-white motion picture film. These colored grains of dye are the basic structure of the image, and what you might call the background noise of the system—like the constant hum, sometimes loud, sometimes almost imperceptible, of a sound system. The finer the grain of the image, the lower its background noise, and the more picture information given.

The human eye-brain mechanism has a similar kind of granular background noise; however, much of the time most of us are not aware of it. You can see it best when your eyes are closed, when the light is dim, or when looking at a flat, textureless area like the sky.

The grain of the motion picture image is more dynamic than the grain of the eye-brain. The random, continually swirling mosaic of color keeps changing because the frames keep changing—24 each second. This moving mosaic, like an animated Seurat, is usually so fine that we pay no attention to it, just as we ignore the granular nature of the visual field.

People sometimes have to down a dose of acid or mescaline before they can perceive this background noise of vision, as the Beatles pointed out in *Lucy in the Sky with Diamonds,* or as Aldous Huxley explained more fully in *The Doors of Perception.* Either by accident or through training, I am generally aware of this scintillating aspect of vision. The clouds of grain of the visual field are closely linked to mandala design. Indeed, the flicker films of Conrad or Kubelka can generate heightened perception of eye-brain grain and produce mandala-like images, despite the fact that these films themselves are totally grainless.

So there is a point of correspondence here, and a very profound one. My perception of *Dog Star Man* and the sky in my yard tie together. Both experiences unleashed a force within me, something which exists in all humans. This force is at the root of visionary experience and artistic creation. Although it was this perception, this phenomenon, that turned me on to filmmaking, only in rare instances do I deal with it directly in my own work, even if these concerns are contained within my films. You see, I am a basement filmmaker because I am attuned to the foundations of the medium. Grain is the mortar of the mansion of film, and the frames are the building blocks. From this perspective, being a basement filmmaker is a positive advantage.

After seven years in the basement, working in 16mm and finishing 18 films, I descended in 1972 to the sub-basement, because it was becoming more difficult to afford to work in 16mm. If it's hard to get a 16mm film distributed, and there is a regular 16mm distribution channel, think of how totally impossible it is to get a super 8 film out to the public, when most of the potential rentors don't even have super 8 projectors. But super 8, because it is less expensive, has allowed me to keep working at a pace I enjoy. I am a prolific filmmaker.

The super 8 image has a substantially different quality from the larger-format 16mm image. It isn't as sharp and isn't as bright, but it's good enough for most purposes. Super 8 has very good sound, and sync-sound super 8 is easy and inexpensive. I have become more of a home moviemaker and a documentarian, which may have been the direction I was going in anyway.

So here I am, in the sub-basement, making movies of my family and friends. The other day I read that *Star Wars* had grossed more than 400 million dollars. I like *Star Wars*. It's a good movie. I saw it three times. George Lucas is in the penthouse and I am in the sub-basement. There are a handful of directors up there with Lucas. There are thousands of filmmakers down here. It's cozy.

Section 1
Polavision

The Polavision system: camera, phototape cassettes, and player.

Polavision, Polaroid Corporation's radically new photographic system, includes a simple-to-use handheld camera, a unique phototape cassette containing two minutes and forty seconds of instant-development, color motion picture film, and a compact tabletop player which presents the vivid-color moving images in seconds.

Introduction:

Will Polavision Be the "Big Mac" of Super 8?

Needham, Massachusetts, April 26, 1977. Nobody could accuse it of being an ordinary day. For this is the day that Dr. Edwin Land, chairman of the board and director of research of Polaroid, demonstrated what the company calls "immediately visible living images." (What they mean is their new "instant" movie system.) And it isn't every day that 3,800 shareholders and members of the press get a chance to film, for eight seconds each, any one of 42 sets (filled with performers) laid out in a football-field-size warehouse that has been emptied of its contents for this event.

An air of near hysteria anticipated this much-awaited product by the crowding of so many souls into this space. That's not to suggest that the event went anything but smoothly. In fact, given the great number of persons and their expectations, one would be hard pressed to orchestrate a better-run participatory event.

The specifications of the Polavision camera may not seem impressive to many die-hard filmmakers. It's a very simple box-type machine running at 18 frames per second (fps) only, with a reflex (through-the-lens) viewfinder, and an automatic exposure meter that cannot be manually overridden. This early model is not a

Dr. Edwin Land introducing Polavision (photo by Bob Doyle, *Super 8 Filmaker*)

sound recording camera, although the silent film "cassette" (Polaroid does not call it a cartridge) does carry magnetically striped film. The camera has a 2:1 zoom ratio with a modest $f/1.8$ lens and far and close focusing ranges. The exposure meter itself is not through-the-lens, but rather an adjacent type, looking through the camera's upper housing.

The Polavision loading door is on the right side, lens facing you, like Fuji single 8 cameras. That's because the film cassette itself more nearly resembles the Fuji cartridge than the Kodak unit. The camera also has an adjustable, par-for-the-course, eyepiece. Power comes from four type AA batteries located in the pistol grip, which a company spokesman claimed would run 50 cassettes. The camera has a built-in type A filter, like all super 8 cameras and recent Fuji single 8 machines, and a plug for a movie light sitting atop the body. Based on my few seconds with the machine, I can tell you that the viewfinder was bright and crisp and the camera comfortable to hold. However, it runs very noisily by the standards I apply to even bottom-of-the-line super 8 equipment.

The film cassette itself resembles the Fuji core-to-core (reel-to-reel) unit, but it is larger than the Fuji device, measuring some 5¼ × 2¾ × ½ inches. Unlike the Fuji cartridge, the Polaroid cassette has a built-in pressure pad much like the Kodak super 8 cartridge.

And unlike both Fuji or Kodak products, the film actually travels from a feed to a take-up reel rather than core-to-core (cores have no side walls). The film within is super 8. However, it is not intended for projection on anything but the Polavision player. The film never leaves the camera cassette, which also serves as the projection cassette. Of course, the cassette, with its maverick dimensions, cannot be used in anything but a Polavision camera. As I mentioned before, the stock is magnetically sound striped so that film shot in a silent camera will not have to be sent back to a lab for striping if the user wants to add narration or music.

I asked Dr. Land if a new cassette that would allow direct sound recording was planned, and whether it could be used with present silent Polavision cameras. He felt that an opening, or port, could be added to the present cassette so that a camera's soundhead could record on the stripe. He said that in all probability, the sound cassette would fit in silent machines, and in time, a single cassette, the sound-ported version, would be offered.

At the moment there is only one film stock available, a type A (balanced for tungsten light) material with an exposure index (EI) of 40, like Kodachrome 40. When used with the built-in daylight filter outdoors, the film has the usual 25 EI. The film contained in the cassette is only about 40 feet long, not the 50 feet we're used to. This plays just about 2½ minutes at 18 fps. The ultra thin emulsion is coated on polyester material, like Fujichrome single 8 film.

The Polavision player is a nearly 12-inch diagonal rear-screen projector the size of a small portable TV. It has only focus and frameline controls. The player offers rapid rewind at about 400 fps, according to Land. When you are finished filming, you insert the cassette in the player, and after a minute and half of processing, the image is projected. Polaroid did not reveal details about where and how the processing was accomplished, and it was not possible to examine any of the equipment zealously guarded by the Polaroid staffers.

It was a great thrill to see movies a minute and a half after you shot them. It's a tremendous selling point, and that's the way all movies ought to be, if you want my opinion. However, there are for now some serious drawbacks to the system. The processed film itself is extremely dense—so dense, in fact, that it cannot be projected with an ordinary super 8 projector. The image would be too dim. That's why the system uses a small rear screen and an intensely bright optical system with a 150-watt lamp.

Given the density difficulty, it's only natural that a bright rear-screen player would have to be employed. The advantage is that the player remains in the living room like a TV set, to be enjoyed without turning the lights out and setting up a screen.

The projected image was bright but extremely grainy, with very high contrast and what I judged in many cases to be washed-out skin tones. I would also call the grain more noticeable than that of any of the fast Ektachrome film stocks now available. However, it was quite difficult to judge the quality since I wasn't conducting tests myself and since the subject matter had been rigged. Forty-two sets with bright backdrops peopled by brightly costumed clowns, dancers, mimes, and jugglers, many of whom wore make-up, made any effort to evaluate the pictorial quality exceedingly difficult.

Despite the fact that the film was very grainy and contrasty, it did appear to be rather sharp, and the colors were very saturated and bright. The image was certainly on a par with a similar-size TV image. However, I noticed marked mottling or blotches of color on a great deal of the footage I inspected, which I assume is due to uneven processing. After testing this product in late 1977, I expected that the defects could be minimized and even cured in time for the full-scale national distribution of Polavision in 1978. (Initial marketing actually started in California the winter of 1977.)

The Polavision system isn't really aimed at serious filmmakers, or even dedicated home moviemakers. It's aimed at people who want to see the unedited version of baby's first step; and they will get to see it almost immediately after filming. It's aimed at people who don't want to edit their film, who want a cassette library of family highlights—picnics, the beloved dog, and so forth. And Polavision is aimed at the TV-acclimated American who is used

Polavision is a home-movie medium, right now, and a Polavision family is a happy family.

to looking at a rear-projected color image in less than optimum conditions in a fully lit room.

Dr. Land may have scored, but are we to take seriously his opinion that he is offering us "a new mechanism for relating to life and each other"? Perhaps he's right; maybe this is, as he put it, "living photography." In a certain sense, I believe Land's hand was forced. After all, each year that goes by, TV tape recording (videotape) gets a little nearer to the consumer home-movie level. The handwriting is on the wall for film if it can't compete with instant tape.

One Step Backward, A Big Step Forward

Edwin Land has repeatedly shown a grasp on technology few can equal. The recent introduction of the Polavision instant movie system is an example of the profound insight the man has on the direction of science and invention. The Polavision system is an eclectic combination of disciplines culled from various physical sciences—optics, chemistry, and mechanical engineering.

All invention is based on past invention, and Land's work has been no exception. His instant photographic systems are developments and refinements of work well known to specialists in the field; however, they lacked Land's ability to perfect the concept.

There is a current running through Land's work which can be traced from his first invention, the Polaroid sheet polarizer. His sheet polarizer has had applications in areas as diverse as scientific instruments, stereoscopic motion picture projection, and photographic filters. Yet Land's achievement, which was accomplished in the late twenties, was based on the work of Dr. William Byrd Herapath, a British scientist who offered the world sheet polarizers in 1852. But it was Land who, three-quarters of a century later, perfected Herapathite, creating a quality product that could be made in large sizes inexpensively.

At the fortieth annual shareholders meeting of the Polaroid Corporation, Land went out of his way to say that it is easier for people to address the negative aspects of a proposed system than the positive qualities. It happens to be a characteristic of the human mind that we are a race of doubting Thomases. But we are also a race of materialistic visionaries, like Thomas Edison, George Eastman, Henry Ford, and Edwin Land.

29

In the Polavision system, a cassette containing 42 feet of super 8 format film is exposed in the camera, then placed in a processing-viewer, to be screened after 90 seconds. The film is processed as it unwinds by 40 drops of a viscous, honeylike reagent. The most amazing part of the process is that it is an additive color system—an obsolete process for many years, at least for consumer photographic products.

The first demonstration of color photography, by the brilliant physicist James Clerk Maxwell, took place in 1861 at the Royal Institution in London. Maxwell employed an additive color system, with red, green, and blue filters made up of colored solutions in glass cells. Through each of these three filters, three photographs were taken. Slides were printed from the negatives, then projected through the filter that had taken the original photo. Maxwell's first color shot was of a scarf. It's not possible to judge the accuracy of the results, but in an absolute sense, the photograph is pleasing.

The idea which is the basis of Land's Polavision system comes to us from Louis Ducos du Hauron, who suggested in 1868 that a layer of color filters arranged in a mosaic pattern be placed over a sensitive emulsion. If an exposure is then made and the emulsion processed as a reversal film, the result can be used as a projected transparency. The drawing here shows the basic scheme of a *screen plate,* as it is called.

Modern color television, with its tube made of a mosaic of phosphors, is an application of du Hauron's idea. Various screen plates have been offered, perhaps the most famous of which was marketed in 1907 by Lumière as the Autochrome plate, which used a random mixture of dyed starch grains (red, green, and blue) squashed into disks overcoating an emulsion.

Other screen plates were known under the brand names of Agfacolor, Dufay, and Padget. You can find examples of photomechanical reproductions made from these plates in issues of *National Geographic* published in the twenties. The soft or pastel rendition of colors and reasonably sharp images are pleasing.

An interesting variation of the screen plate bearing a direct relationship to the present Polavision system is the Dufay plate, which was available through the fifties, if I am not mistaken. The

Cross sections of phototape in action.

1. Film exposed to light through polyester base. Silver grains in negative layer have been exposed—to red light in our example—and are ready for development. The emulsion is not exposed behind the green and blue filters in additive layer.

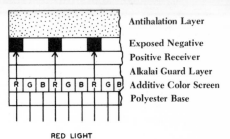

Antihalation Layer

Exposed Negative
Positive Receiver
Alkalai Guard Layer
Additive Color Screen
Polyester Base

RED LIGHT

2. Developing reagent spreads evenly across the antihalation layer and permeates top layers, but is stopped by guard layer. The reagent starts to bleach the antihalation dyes, necessary at the time of photography to prevent reflection of light from rear of film. After processing, antihalation dyes would make the image too dense, so they must go.

Exposed silver in negative layer is developed while undeveloped silver migrates to positive layer which, in conjunction with reagent, creates a positive image.

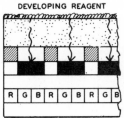

DEVELOPING REAGENT

Antihalation Layer

Exposed and Developing
Negative
Positive Image Forming
Alkalai Guard Layer
Additive Color Screen
Polyester Base

3. When light is projected through the film, the positive image layer blocks the light from passing through any but the red filter elements in our example. Although the negative layer remains, it is much less dense than the positive layer and does not contribute to image formation. However, it does prevent a portion of the light from reaching the screen, as must the additive filters. Polavision can only be rear projected on a small screen.

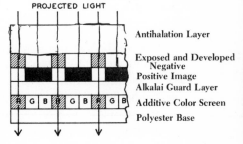

PROJECTED LIGHT

Antihalation Layer

Exposed and Developed
Negative
Positive Image
Alkalai Guard Layer
Additive Color Screen
Polyester Base

screen was made up of cross-hatched lines ruled or printed on the base in the red, green, and blue series like today's color TV screen. The Polavision system also uses a system of rulings, and their formation must have presented a formidable technical problem, since an ultra fine pattern of parallel ruling was necessary for the small super 8 format.

In essence, the Polavision film is a black-and-white emulsion, exposed through its base. Light reaching the emulsion is filtered by a series of red, blue, and green rulings, as shown in the drawing. The processed film, a positive image, is projected on the face of a rear-screen viewer. It seems obvious that this kind of an additive process is simpler to bring off than a more complex subtractive process, like Ektachrome movie film.

It's called an *additive* process because individual components of colored light are added together on the surface of the screen to form a full-color image. In the case of Maxwell's original demonstration, light from three appropriately filtered slides had been mixed on top of each other. For the Polavision process, or for color TV, adjacent elements—spots of red, blue, and green light—are projected for the eye to blend into an image of continuous colors.

The *subtractive* process, used in all modern color transparency and negative films, uses three layers of film dyed to make up the full-color image. The various densities of the dyes filter (or subtract) the light projected through them. It's rather amazing that a complex sandwich of layers of emulsions, dyes, and filters can produce the quality and consistency we all expect and get from color films.

You can think of the difference between the Polavision additive color system and the usual subtractive systems, like Kodachrome for example, in this way: Polavision is like pointillism, which constructed images out of dots of color that the eye blended into recognizably mixed colors at an adequate distance. Subtractive color films are like conventional painting techniques, in which the colors are blended on the palette before applying them to canvas.

But additive color has serious defects. The filters reduce the light needed for exposure and greatly lower film speed. Upon projection, a great deal of light is similarly lost, making for dim images. Making prints from additive-to-additive stock could also prove troublesome, since moiré (or gridlike) patterns would be produced. Of course I would imagine that a film like Polavision can be printed on an Ektachrome-type print stock with success.

These drawbacks in the additive system led to flagging interest in the process, and to the perfection of subtractive films. But Dr. Land reasoned that the advantages of the system, for the Polavision application, outweighed the disadvantages. It's easier to process black-and-white film than a subtractive color film, and Polavision takes advantage of this.

Right now the major disadvantage of additive Polavision is that the film must be shown on a small rear screen, because of filter light absorption. The negative image layer also remains after processing and blocks a substantial portion of the light. (An adjacent positive-image receiving layer is the recipient of unexposed silver from the processing negative layer. These migrated silver grains become the positive image, but the negative grains remain to block light in the negative layer.) Also, the grain and filter pattern, while not obtrusive, was noticeable in the introductory demonstration shown to the press and shareholders. This would seem to preclude projection on large screens since the pattern itself would become even more visible. So the question remains: Is it possible to overcome the disadvantages of additive color Polavision?

One thing is very interesting about this instant photographic system. All future changes in film and processing can be enclosed in the Polavision cassette, without alerting the user or nonexistent processing labs. The self-contained film and processing lab enclosed in each cassette allows for tremendous freedom on the part of the manufacturer in terms of improving or even radically altering the product. It's even possible that the cassette now housing Polavision could be used to contain a subtractive process.

I happen to think that the future of photography is quite obviously going in the direction of instant systems, and that the Polavision process, by taking one step backward to additive color, has actually taken us a giant step forward.

A User Report

It's been a pleasure to test the Polavision system. It isn't so much that I'm blindly in love with Land's new instant moving image system; it's just that I've relished the opportunity to evaluate this mighty interesting toy. For years now, as a filmmaker and a writer specializing in motion picture technology, I've had a chance to check out many tools. For sheer fascination, this one takes the prize. It's the most original product I've come up against, and I've enjoyed the challenge.

Despite the fact that Polavision is aimed at the unsophisticated user, I can't avoid bringing to bear my own sensibility and expertise. So while I make no bones about the subjective nature of this report, I will, as the occasion warrants, bring to mind the most likely user and his or her possible relationship with the equipment.

The Polavision system relies on two major pieces of hardware—a camera and a player—and the software of the system—the self-processing phototape. The camera, which is designed to be as automatic as possible, lists for $184, and the unadorned player costs $515. Together they total $699 list, but everyone is aware that merchandise like this is often discounted at from 10 to 20 percent in many shops (the three I checked in northern California confirmed this).

The Camera

The Polavision Land movie camera is an example of modern industrial design, and the most important consideration about any such

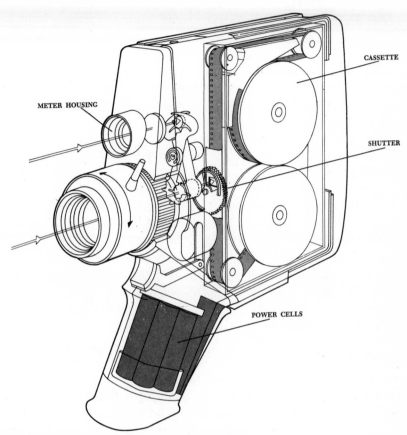

CASSETTE

METER HOUSING

SHUTTER

POWER CELLS

The Polavision camera is conventional in design.

design, from the maker's point of view, is to generate a buying urge in the consumer. How to make a camera to appeal to a mass market? The Polavision designers have taken a middle course, somewhere between Kodak machines so cozy they almost deny their function and products from many factories that pile on the knobs and dials in an attempt to appeal to the demented passions of the fanatic. While the sturdy Polavision camera body itself has elegantly slim lines, the effect is spoiled by the rough-textured, blunt-shaped pistol grip which undercuts the original intention. The lens housing at the front of the camera is also too busy to work with the nice lines of the body.

All told, however, I'd say the Polavision designers have scored. This chintzy injection-molded camera will probably appeal to many people who respond favorably to discordant elements. But, it's all a question of taste, right? Having disposed of form, onward to function.

There's an $f/1.8$, 12.5 to 25mm zoom lens, a through-the-lens non-focusing finder, and an automatic light meter with a sensor that sees through a housing sitting above the lens. The lens focuses for two positions only, near and far. Near is 6 to 15 feet, and far stretches from there to infinity. Each symbol, 6′–15′ or 15′–∞, appears below the finder image when you've made your choice. There's a battery test button, a window that tells you if film is in the camera, a film indicator that tells you if your film is ¼, ½, ¾, or F for finished, and a sliding lock that lets you open the door so that you may insert or remove a cartridge. The grip contains four AA cells, which will drive a great many cassettes. A movie light, which they call the TwiLight, attaches to the top of the camera for indoor filming.

The camera balances very nicely, and feels good to use. The finder is bright and crisp. In addition to the focusing readout, it has a big black pointer for underexposure alert, and it displays a red flash seconds before you run out of film.

When holding the grip, the web of the thumb depresses the electrical safety switch, and the trigger itself is depressed by the index finger. The camera runs noisier than I'd like. Actually, it's about as loud as my 4008 Beaulieu. Well, they're both too loud. The loading chamber slide switch has to be pressed into place to lock the door. Most simple movie cameras automatically lock once the door is closed. It's another thing to remember, a small one to be sure, but I'd prefer not to have to think about it.

The automatic meter is easily fooled by backlight situations. There is no backlight control, which is unfortunate. However, by holding your finger across the cell itself, say covering half of it, you can make the diaphragm open up a stop or so. This is important to know, since even a sliver of bright sky in the composition can cause the automatic system to stop down the lens far too much, resulting in ruinous underexposures. The phototape itself has very little exposure latitude, so exposures have to be right on the button.

The major—no, the only—accessory at this time is the TwiLight, which mounts to the top of the camera but is powered by a cord which plugs into the bottom of the body from the electric power outlet. The TwiLight is neatly designed, producing very bright light with little heat from two quartz lamps with built-in reflectors that resemble many projector lamps. Being so fiercely bright, people can't help but squint when you depress the safety on the rear of the grip.

When the TwiLight is added to the camera, the built-in daylight conversion filter is automatically swung out of the lens. Since phototape is balanced for artificial light, the filter must be in place when shooting outdoors, but it is not needed when using the TwiLight.

I tried closeups using a plus 1 lens, and got good results at about 3 feet from the camera. Polaroid will probably offer such an accessory lens sooner or later, but you can buy one now at any good camera shop.

People like to get into their own movies, and Polaroid has seriously goofed by not incorporating a locking trigger, a cable release, or a remote control feature so that the camera can be left running. Now if you want to get into the shot or leave an unattended camera running, you can tape, tie, or rubber-band the electric safety and trigger —if the camera is tripod mounted. Not convenient, but certainly possible.

The camera's images are very sharp most of the time, indicating that the designers have not cut corners with the optics. It's a pleasant and easy-to-use machine, and for those who use it, it will undoubtedly produce a high percentage of good images. The most serious flaw is the lack of backlight control. One cure would be to bias the meter's sensitivity to the bottom of the composition, away from the sky.

Sophisticated filmmakers, who seek all kinds of controls and doodads, will do well to adjust their ambitions to the limitations of the design. Having said this, let me add that I would be much happier with a different zoom range, say 7 to 14mm, instead of the 12.5 to

25mm the designers chose. These are rather long focal lengths, making too narrow a field of view for general snapshooting.

The machine appears to be sturdy, even robust, and produces good images; but by conventional super 8 standards, it's got a high price tag. The list of $184 is justified to a large extent by the instantness of the system.

The Player

The Polavision looks like a small TV with an 11¾-inch diagonal screen on which images are rear projected. The player is also the processing machine in that it provides the drive for the processing, which takes place in the cassette. A slot on the top is just about the only break in the featureless brown body of the unit. Drop in the cassette, press lightly, and the processing of a freshly exposed film is underway. In about a minute and a half, the image appears on the screen. That's it, as far as the user is concerned. You don't add chemicals or anything. Nothing to clean up or throw away. Just put the player on a table, plug it in, drop in the cassette, and in a very short while indeed, you see your movies.

Near the fold-down carrying handle there is a focusing control, and at the back, a frameline control. The power cord stores in a hatch in the rear, which also gives access to the 150-watt low-voltage lamp. There is also an eject button at the rear of the machine; depressing it causes the cassette to pop up even in the middle of projection. A hatch on the bottom allows the inside mirrors to be cleaned. (Don't touch; use canned compressed air or a blower-syringe.)

The projected image is sharp and adequately bright. However, image brilliance seems to fall off more rapidly than with other rear-screen units in common use. The player runs very noisily. Apparently there has been no attempt to engineer quietness either in the player or camera. This is characteristic of the super 8 industry in general, but Polaroid seems to have gone overboard.

Given the implicit design philosophy and the audience for the product, the omission that I can't understand is the lack of a slow motion feature. People often like to look at their silent movies in

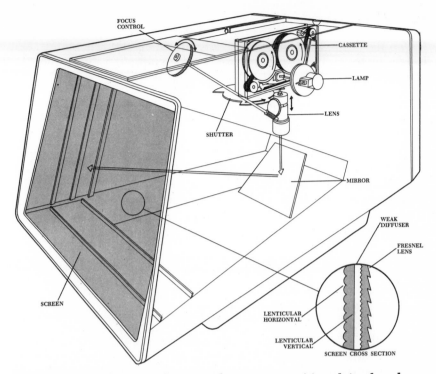

FOCUS
CONTROL

CASSETTE

LAMP

LENS

SHUTTER

MIRROR

WEAK
DIFFUSER

FRESNEL
LENS

SCREEN

LENTICULAR
HORIZONTAL

LENTICULAR
VERTICAL

SCREEN CROSS SECTION

The Polavision player is shown with cassette positioned in the player for projection. Note screen cross section inset. The screen is actually a three-lens-and-diffuser affair, with Fresnel lens and horizontal and vertical elements to make the most out of the 150-watt lamp. The light passes through the Fresnel lens making the light rays parallel, then through the lenticular screens that spread the beam both horizontally and vertically to fill what is assumed to be a decent angle of view. While this may result in a fairly bright central image, at the sides of the screen the image is dim.

slow motion, which they can do with just about every other super 8 silent projector, front or rear screen.

There is a remote accessory, the instant replay control, which plugs into the rear of the machine. Depress it and the film winds back and the last few seconds are replayed. It's a nice touch, and adds one more element to a design which has been heavily tempered by the television medium. The player is more like a TV to most folks than a movie projector. That leads to an expectation of sound. This lack, it turns out, is the most missed component cited by people who give the system a once-over-lightly. But that's like criticizing an apple for not tasting like an orange—or is it?

The $515 list for the player is high, in my view, given the context of quality already present in rear-screen units, like those from Eumig and Bolex, which are much less expensive and have many more features. (Both the Polavision camera and player, by the way, are manufactured in Vienna in the Eumig factory, which is known for making good equipment.) Once again, the consumer is being asked to pay for the instantness of the product. You have to decide whether it's worth your money.

Phototape

As mentioned, Polaroid calls its rapid processing film *phototape* (type 608). It is actually super 8 perforated format stock, but very thin. Film usually has perfs, and tape doesn't. However, film usually has far more body. Phototape is a very thin (but strong) polyester material. So one could argue that we do have a kind of tape housed in the cassette. But what's in a name? Film by any other name would record the same.

The cassette, containing the phototape, is a neat gadget: It houses the film for camera and player, and it also serves as a processing lab. Contained within it are 40 drops of gooey liquid used for processing the film when the cassette is placed in the player for the first time. For projection, light is beamed through the film by a plastic prism coated with a metallic reflecting layer housed in the cassette. It's a very efficient system.

As mentioned, the phototape, or film, has the same speed and filtration as Kodachrome 40, which is used by most super 8 film-makers. I shot a gray scale and color chart, provided by DeLuxe Laboratories. The gray scale runs from black to white in seven steps. The color patches are labeled red, green, blue, yellow, cyan, and magenta. Everybody is familiar with these colors except cyan,

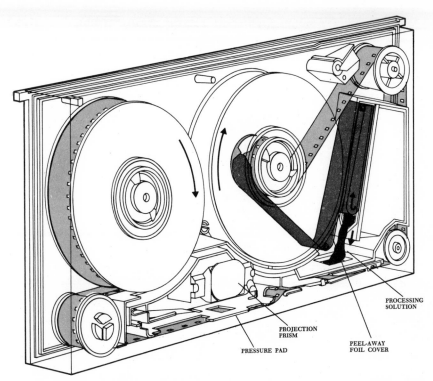

PROCESSING
SOLUTION

PROJECTION
PRISM

PEEL-AWAY
FOIL COVER

PRESSURE PAD

The Polavision cassette performs three functions: it houses the film and assists during exposure, processing, and projection. Pressure pad positions film during both exposure and playback, when light is angled through prism. As first rewind begins, the film peels a foil cover from a small cavity, releasing a small amount of viscous reagent. The film gets coated with a very thin layer of this liquid as it passes through a molded slot and rewinds on the supply reel at 400 feet per minute.

which is a more or less sky blue, and magenta, which could be called a pink red. I conducted the tests for both daylight and tungsten, using the TwiLight accessory.

Filmed and projected, the phototape was able to reproduce only four or five steps of the gray scale (Kodachrome can do all seven). I was able to move the exposure up or down by covering part of the meter sensor with my finger or by inserting a white card into the sensor's field of view behind the gray scale. Although I didn't know what f stop I was at, I could see the results of, say, a stop under or over exposure. The gray scale was reproduced more or less neutrally, slightly on the warm side. Although its neutrality was pleasing, the high contrast and limited exposure latitude (far less than conventional super 8 materials) revealed itself in this test.

The color patches were also far less accurately reproduced than is usually the case with conventional emulsions. Red, yellow, and magenta seemed to hold up the best. The red wasn't as brilliant as it ought to have been, the yellow was pleasing but on the orange side, and the magenta was most accurately reproduced. Yellow washed out very quickly with only a little bit of overexposure.

Green reproduced poorly; it was muddy. Reproduction of blue and cyan was adequate, although there was insufficient distinction between the two and cyan tended to look dull.

In the field, things looked much better. Skin tones, which are most important, were pleasing. Textiles also reproduced nicely. Blue skies were okay but not especially brilliant, as we have come to expect. Green leaves and grass were often adequate, but just a little bit of underexposure was enough to rob foliage's vitality. As my yardstick of comparison, I've used conventional super 8 materials like Kodachrome. But it might make just as much sense to use color TV as the standard, in which case Polavision fares very well. Most people will be pleased by the color, but there's a great deal of room for improvement.

The film is too contrasty for my taste. Shadow detail tended to get obliterated, even with the uniform illumination of an overcast day. Highlights on light-colored objects were burnt out, which is what I would have expected from the reproduction of the gray scale chart. (Actually, I shot the charts last.) A lower-contrast material with a longer tonal scale and improved exposure latitude is needed.

The film is very, very sharp. It gets high marks for this. It's probably as sharp or sharper than conventional materials, and, to my eye, much sharper than TV. But the film is also exceedingly grainy, and although many users may not be terribly concerned with this, I think it's only borderline acceptable. Even the fastest super 8 emulsions have finer grain when projected on small screens. The grain is probably caused by a fast emulsion hiding behind bands of color filters. Remember the film is an additive process, and a triad array of ruled red, green, and blue lines are overlaid on the emulsion. They probably absorb a quarter of the light. The emulsion behind them must be equivalent to an EI of about 200, and fast emulsions are more granular than slow emulsions. Or the apparent granularity may be a negative synergistic effect, combining the usual photographic grain with the fixed color raster, or striped pattern (plus the lenticular screen of the player), which in and of itself is hard to see. It is certainly an astonishing technical feat that such a fine raster can be produced in an assembly-line product.

The overall registration, or image steadiness, of the system—camera, phototape, and player—is adequate, but that, too, could warrant improvement. The image quality is very similar to film as seen over a film chain. That's probably because of the fixed raster overlaid on each frame, which is very much like the phosphor pattern used in the Sony color TV tubes.

About a third of the cassettes I used had serious glitches, or areas of picture information dropout. These lasted for several seconds and appeared as annoying gray patches. Also, there was a subtle effect of changing density produced no doubt by uneven processing, which sometimes had the appearance of mottling or water marks toward the edges of the frame.

Having found these faults with the product, let me say that overall I am actually pleased and even excited with the results. I think most folks, who are undoubtedly going to have a point of view different from mine, will probably find the technical aspects to be of less importance than the creative problems they will face with this new medium. How will they go about shooting cassettes (which cannot be edited) of their family and friends that will remain interesting for repeated viewings?

I must point out that I am critizing the first batches of phototape to reach the public, and that it would be reasonable to expect considerable improvement in the months to come.

Projecting Polavision on Big Screens

Polavision was meant to be projected on the Polavision player, and the player only. First of all, the film is housed in a cassette that will fit into nothing but the player. In the second place, the phototape image intself is terrifically dense. Even if you took it out of the cassette, you'd need a very bright projector. And third, the polyester base material is thin and has far less body than the usual super 8 material for which projectors have been designed. It might have trouble being advanced in conventional machines.

There are times, however, when the usefulness of Polavision could be greatly extended if it could be shown on a larger screen to a greater number of people than can crowd around the nearly 12-inch diagonal player screen. From time to time, I teach film-making in the classroom, and if the Polavision system were used there, it could help students learn how to properly handle a camera. In this application, it would be better, I feel, to project on a big screen. At any rate, one of the positive advantages of film, as compared with video, is that it can be displayed on large screens with very little effort or expense. Can we gain this advantage for Polavision?

The answer is yes, naturally, or I wouldn't be writing this. First you've got to get the film out of the cassette—*after it's been processed.* You'll notice that there is a circular depression, or dimple, on the cassette immediately adjacent to the circular prism opening. You've got to drill out that dimple with a ⅛-inch (or slightly larger) drill bit. Next, using a knife, slit the yellow and blue label along the entire length of its edge on the side of the cassette opposite where you drilled. By examining the join of the two halves of the cassette, you'll find several convenient places to insert the knife edge. Gently pry the cassette halves apart.

Once you've removed the cassette cover, you'll see the two spools of film within. You must wind the phototape off the spools onto a conventional super 8 spool. In the processing of Polavision, a caustic chemical agent is used, and opening the cassette makes it possible for you to come in contact with it, if there's any left.

I opened two cassettes that had been shot and processed a week before, and there was no evidence of anything wet within. But the presence of any caustic agent is more likely in a freshly processed cassette, and suitable precautions should be taken.

Once you've got the phototape on a conventional super 8 reel, add some leader to help the film thread through the projector. You probably noticed the extreme density of the phototape image. The base side, which has laminated magnetic stripe and balance stripe, appears to be purplish by reflected light, and the emulsion side looks like film that has been developed but not left in the hypo long enough. If you hold the film up to the light, you'll see frames appearing dimly through a dense violet background. If you put the phototape in a viewer, you'll find that only a dim image is visible, probably ruling out editing with conventional equipment. However, tape splices may be made, and they will pass through a suitable projector, or the player, with no trouble.

Now we're up to threading the film on a projector. In my studio I tried several Eumig sound models and the silent Kodak Moviedeck 477. The Eumigs would not pass the phototape; they kept losing the loop. But the Moviedeck had no trouble with the phototape. If I am to generalize on what happened, based on experiments with three machines, I'd say that phototape, because it's so very thin, will have trouble on conventional sprocket drive machines but will work on sprocketless drive machines like the Kodak Moviedeck. Sprocketless drive is just what it sounds like: no sprockets, but rather tape-recorder-type rollers or snubbers to help transport the film.

You can view the phototape on the built-in Moviedeck screen, which is about 3½ X 5 inches, or much smaller than the player screen. This would be interesting if you wanted to use the fast or slow motion features of the 477 (it runs at 54, 18, 6, and 3 fps, and still frame; 18 fps gives normal motion).

To project on a big screen, you need the Ektalite model 3, a 40-inch-wide screen of very high-grain properties. In a well-darkened room, the Moviedeck 477 can project an image of adequate brightness on this screen, which bears a strong resemblance to the large-screen TV images projected by the VideoBeam made by the Advent Corporation. Of course the images may be shown at slow or fast motion, and many more people can look at the movies than would have been possible had you used the player. I was quite frankly surprised that the image was as bright as it was, for I felt discouraged as I examined the phototape fresh out of the cassette. I thought that it was too dense, but having gone that far with it, I took it the rest of the way and projected on the Ektalite.

The results on the big screen were quite good. As I have said, the image looks more like large-screen TV than movies, or like a movie that has been broadcast on TV and shown on a large screen. The color stripes became more visible, while they were almost unnoticeable on the player screen, and the granularity of the image was obvious. The colors, which can be quite brilliant on the player screen, were less saturated but entirely acceptable on the large screen, and the image remained quite sharp. I got a kick out of looking at these images on a bigger screen, and I feel certain that this approach could greatly extend the utility of the system. (Several months after this was written, Land demonstrated large-screen Polavision projection, using a somewhat similar scheme.)

If a sound projector were used, say a sprocketless drive unit like the Canon PS 1000 (if it works with phototape), sound could also be added to the image, since the phototape is striped.

If you want to put the phototape back into the cassette so that you can look at it on the player, you may be out of luck. It looks like a very difficult procedure to reload the cassette so that it will function properly. However, there are probably people out there with the requisite skill to pull it off. If so, a viable approach to editing might also be found, since phototape removed could be cut and then restored to the cassette for projection with the player.

Section 2

Super 8: Tools for Making the Image

Introduction:

Cameras and Other Loves

Since I was a little kid my heart has been set ablaze by cameras and lenses. If I hadn't needed to use my old camera or lens as a trade-in item to buy something new that caught my fancy, I'd still be the proud possessor of a Kodak Pony 135, a Leica IIIb, a Contax IIA, and an Angenieux 9.5 to 95mm lens. And there were, of course, others; so many, but who can remember them all?

Among the fraternity of filmmakers there is a large number of equipment freaks, who would much rather pet and fondle and rap about their cameras than shoot a foot of film. Or better yet, feel how sweet it is to drool about some passionately desired, stupendously priced camera they would buy if they only had the bucks. Well, fellas and gals, if that's your persuasion, there is certainly something in the following section for you.

If on the other hand you admire good tools without necessarily worshipping them, viewing them primarily as a means to an end, there's even more of interest for you.

The Truth Behind
the XL Camera Boom

Although I've written about XL filmmaking in the past, I've skirted the challenging question of what the photographic industry means by the acronym XL. The term XL stands for *existing light* (or maybe extra light), and is generally applied to cameras with the ability to shoot in low light or existing light conditions (for example, under artificial lighting indoors without the help of photofloods). But what is actually meant by existing light—and how many cameras labeled XL really conform to a true XL standard?

Let's first take the question of what existing light means in terms of filmmaking. Given an XL camera with its fast lens, usually $f/1.2$, and its broad shutter angle of 220 degrees or thereabouts, you should be able to get good exposures even in a measly 5 foot-candles of incident light when you shoot with a fast film like Ektachrome G.

And what, might you ask, are 5 foot-candles of incident light? Why, that's how much light you have when your *incident* light-meter reads 5 on its scale. An incident meter measures light coming from the light source, rather than light reflected by the subject you're filming (as do light meters built into most cameras). The source light measurement is based on an actual standard "candle" which, when burned, is supposed to produce 1 foot-candle of illumination when measured a foot from the flame. (Actually, what is measured isn't a candle at all, but rather the light emitted by a crucible of molten platinum under certain specified conditions.) Five of these unit candles will produce the intensity that is the minimum illumination required by the modern XL system for good exposures using fast (160 EI) color reversal stock.

To give you some sort of idea what this measure means, about 5,000 foot-candles would be what you'd measure outdoors on a sunny day. Five to ten foot-candles is a pretty representative figure for your typical artificially illuminated kitchen or living room at night.

However, and here's the rub, many cameras given the XL name really don't conform to this standard. Here's a testing procedure you can use to definitely establish whether or not a camera actually can take good exposures with 5 foot-candles of light. Or at least it's a way to determine comparative exposure levels of various cameras. Illuminate an 18 percent Kodak neutral gray test card, sold for exposure test purposes by most large photographic dealers, with 5 foot-candles of light. (You'll need to use a hand-held incident meter to get the light just right.) Then shoot the card with your test cameras wide open at an exposure reading of $f/1.2$. The cameras should be running at the same speed (18 or 24 fps). Measure the density of the processed test film with a densitometer, or compare the density of the exposure by eyeball, and you'll know soon enough which cameras are the fastest.

It seems obvious that the industry could adopt such a standard, and that cameras could be objectively rated in terms of their actual foot-candle capability. I, for one, would like to see this happen. Perhaps the Society of Motion Picture and Television Engineers (SMPTE) should concern themselves about these standards. You'd expect the industry itself to be concerned about false claims of XL capability. I'll do my part here and now by attempting to educate the buying public to the facts in the "Great XL Race."

One could be generous and say that since standards do not exist, manufacturers claiming XL capability for cameras which don't meet the 5 foot-candle standard can't be blamed for their enthusiastic or dishonest claims. It's an open joke that a growing number of cameras labeled XL with $f/1.7$ or $f/1.8$ lenses, light-absorbing broad zoom ranges, viewfinder optics, and behind-the-lens meters have one, and only one, claim to being XL—the broad

220-degree shutter angle. This shutter lets more light through to the film than the usual 170-degree shutter found on super 8 production cameras.

However, there's much more to XL capability than merely having a 220-degree shutter, since a standard production camera with *only* this addition of a 220-degree shutter is going to gain about 30 or 40 percent in exposure, or hardly half a stop. But true XL machines have a healthy two or three stop improvement in exposure. So don't be fooled. Nobody can make a camera with an $f/1.8$ lens that's as fast as a camera with an $f/1.2$ lens. Can't be done. If low-light capability is what you crave most of all, stay away from these shucks, which, sad to say, are being brought to you by a few of your most reputable manufacturers. These folks should know better, since in some cases they are also making true XL cameras.

I've been working with two XL cameras, and they are both capable performers in the 5 foot-candle range. One is the Kodak XL362 with an $f/1.2$, 9 to 21mm Ektar lens, and the other is the Minolta XL-400 with an $f/1.2$, 8.4 to 34mm Rokkor lens. Both cameras have first-rate optics. They are crisp and contrasty and just about everything you'd expect from a modern lens. (The XL-400 has been superseded by the similar XL-401 shown in the photo here. The comparison remains valid.)

The Kodak machine departs from the traditional concept of camera design and handles like a pair of binoculars. In terms of finish and trim, Kodak makes good textural use of plastic and metal; I find that to be very pleasing. The Minolta design is an attempt to make a smartly styled camera that has the look of traditional quality. When all is said and done, the esthetic of actually holding and feeling the instrument is as important a consideration of how XLish the camera is as its various features.

In terms of features, the Minolta has it over the Kodak camera. The Minolta XL-400 has a built-in intervalometer for low frames-per-second settings, in addition to its normal 18-fps speed. It also has a PC flash outlet for double-system sync, a macro zoom lens for extreme closeups, and f stops which can be set manually, while the Kodak XL362 has a meter lock to hold the desired setting.

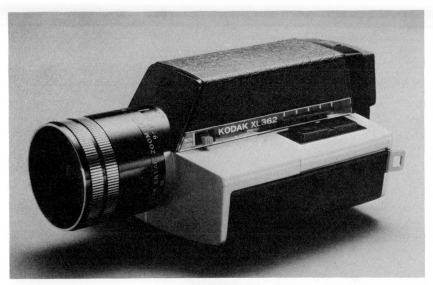

Kodak XL362.

It also has a separate motor for the power zoom, while the Minolta takes its power zoom by gearing off the drive motor. Practically speaking, this means that the Minolta's power zoom cannot be used when the camera isn't running.

Probably the major feature difference is that the Kodak machine uses an adjacent-type viewfinder and the Minolta uses a through-the-lens reflex viewing system with split-image focusing. Whichever is better is up to you and your eyeball. The Kodak machine, with its simpler optics and viewfinder and external meter for exposures, is probably one-third or a quarter stop faster than the Minolta, at least on paper.

There are dozens of other XL designs to choose from. Certainly the choice extends beyond the Minolta XL-400 and the Kodak XL362, although they would be good choices for many readers. In the dozen years since super 8 was first introduced, there have been two major advances—sound-on-film, or single-system, cameras, and XL cameras. (Single system means sound and images are recorded on one machine.) Even though it's like comparing

Minolta XL-401

the proverbial apples and oranges, of the two, the XL feature is more important to my way of looking at things. After all, if you can't produce a well-exposed image, who needs sync sound?

Beyond XL

Have you read about Stanley Kubrick's use of a special Zeiss $f/0.7$, 50mm lens for shooting a great deal of his film *Barry Lyn-*

don? The lens had been designed for the space program, and Kubrick, one of the few theatrical directors deeply interested in the technical aspects of filmmaking, had a 35mm studio camera modified to accept the lens. If you've seen *Barry Lyndon,* you may recall the candlelight sequences, filmed with the fast lens. Despite what must have been extremely limited depth of field, the images were very crisp. Kubrick also employed a special afocal converter to reduce the focal length of the lens to a wider 35mm. Roughly, a 50mm lens for the 35mm format has the same coverage as a 12mm lens in super 8, and a 35mm focal length lens is the equivalent of an 8mm lens in super 8.

Reading about all of that got me thinking about the super 8 XL system, and how far beyond its present low-light capacity we might reasonably expect it to go if some determined manufacturer took on the challenge. Right now, your run-of-the-mill XL camera, loaded with 160 ASA film, can take pictures in about 5 foot-candles of light. Kubrick's $f/0.7$ lens is a stop and a half, or three times faster than the $f/1.2$ XL lens. A super 8 camera with such a lens and a 220-degree shutter could make pictures in about 1 or 2 foot-candles. If some enterprising manufacturer offered a super 8 camera with, say, a $f/0.7$, 10mm lens, I'll bet there'd be a ready market for the product—if not among filmmakers, then within the ranks of private eyes, the FBI, and other people who have to see in the dark to make a living.

Right now, you can switch to a faster film, say black-and-white Tri-X, which is more than twice as sensitive to light as the fast Ektachromes, if you want to take pictures in a couple of foot-candles. You can also have any of the fast Ektachromes pushed a stop, but your film will show a marked increase in grain. These same fast or pushed films in the XXL camera with its $f/0.7$ lens could take pictures in less than a foot-candle.

Century Wide-Angle Lenses

I recently had an opportunity to use two lenses which could greatly extend photographic possibilities for super 8 filmmakers.

Generally, super 8 cameras fitted with noninterchangeable zoom optics have a minimum focal length of not less than 6 or 7mm. If these focal lengths are considered to be wide angle, then the new Century Precision lenses surely qualify as ultra wide-angle lenses. A few super 8 fixed zoom models, like the Eumig PC cameras, offer a wide-angle component which may be fitted to the front of the camera to shorten the focal length to an effective 4mm. Ehrenreich Photo-Optical Industries also offer the Aspheron attachment for Bolex 581 and 551 XL sound cameras. Another prime "C" mount interchangeable lens of short focal length is the 5.5mm lens offered by Fuji.

Long focal lengths have never been much of a problem for super 8 cinematography, since many of the zoom lenses offer focal lengths in the 40 to 80mm range, and those cameras accepting "C" mount thread optics will accept any one of literally hundreds of long lenses designed for 16mm camera bodies. But the area most in need of attention has been the short focal length or wide-angle end of the lens spectrum.

Attempting to fill this gap now are the $f/1.8$ Century Precision 2.5 and 3.5mm wide-angle optics. Since they are "C" mount lenses, they will fit the Fujica 1000, the various Beaulieu cameras, or the Pathé double super 8 machine.

The 3.5mm lens, which costs $450, is the more compact of the two, as well as the more generally useful. The bulkier 2.5mm, costing $595, is a very extreme focal length, useful in all probability for only special shots.

Since so many of us have experience with 35mm still cameras and their interchangeable optics, it may be useful to specify the approximate equivalents of the two lenses in terms we are familiar with, although the shape of the super 8 and 35mm still frames are different. The super 8 frame is squarer than the elongated still frame (the aspect ratio is 1.3 versus 1.5). The 3.5, then, is the rough equivalent of a 21mm optic, and the 2.5 the rough equivalent of a 15mm still lens.

For this test, I used a Beaulieu 4008 camera, and I had some problems obtaining really sharp images with these lenses, especially the 2.5mm wide open, say at $f/1.8$ to $f/2.8$. I believe the problem here was the short depth of focus, which is measured at the film plane. In other words, for producing sharp images, the distance between the lens and film is especially critical for wide-angle optics. While depth of field is measured in the space of the objects being photographed, depth of focus is measured at the film plane; essentially it is a specifiable engineering tolerance for positioning the lens with respect to film.

Bill Turner, sales manager of Century, tells me that they will individually adjust, or collimate, each lens to match the specific camera you plan to use. They'll need your camera for this operation, which involves fitting the lens to the body and making minute adjustments to the distance the lens sits from the film plane. Once the lens is set up in this manner, the maximum focusing potential of the optic will be ensured for that particular camera.

As received with the lens wide open, objects close to the camera, say half a meter away, were very sharp. (A meter is about 40 inches.) Stopping down (using a numerically higher f stop) indicated that the performance of the lens ought to be very good if properly collimated to the body. I say this because depth of focus, like depth of field, increases as the lens is closed down. As these lenses came out of the box, sharp images were obtained wide open for objects less than a meter from the camera. But stopped down, they were good for greater distances.

The shorter of the two, the 2.5mm, tended to have a great deal of curvilinear distortion, or outward bowing of vertical and horizontal lines, toward the edges of the field. Barrel distortion was more subdued for the 3.5mm lens. If you were planning to use a wide-angle optic like the 2.5mm for, say, architectural work, you would not be using the lens to its best advantage, since the resultant distortion would be objectionable in this context. For general photography, though, the image I think would be just fine, the optical effect tending to heighten what most folks have come to accept as an extreme wide-angle "look." In other words, when using an extreme wide-angle lens, the filmmaker undoubtedly wants to create a special effect, and the 2.5mm will supply it. However, the 2.5mm shouldn't be confused with a fisheye lens: although the design may be similar, the effect is not so extreme.

The 3.5mm is a true wide-angle lens which can be employed to good purpose more often for more situations. Its lighter weight and smaller size than the $f/1.8$, 6 to 66mm Schneider, which I usually use on my Beaulieu 4008, appreciably changed the way I handled the camera. It made a pleasant package that encouraged a great deal of shooting, especially casual home movies, since no focusing was required. The lens was particularly suitable for shooting indoors, in the home, in confined spaces. I consider it to be one of the most useful lenses I have used. These optics are available only from the manufacturer, Century, at 10661 Burbank Blvd., N. Hollywood, California 91601.

Power to Spare

I've found that often it's of great importance to use auxiliary power when operating a super 8 camera. This is especially true with single-system sound cameras which have a greater need for current than silent machines. Beyond the demands made by the power zoom motor, the automatic diaphragm system, and the film transport motor, single-system sound machines need power to run the capstan motor that drives the film past the soundhead parts. Also, power operates the control circuitry stabilizing the relationship between the film transport and capstan motor. And let's not forget that sound cameras have amplifiers that require power too.

What generally happens first when power begins to diminish is loused-up sound quality, usually in the form of marked wow and flutter, or the gargling, chirping sound pointing out a lack of constancy in the rate of the capstan motor. Often batteries that test out okay at the start of a cartridge can fail midway through a 50-foot run. If you have sharp ears, you can hear the faltering sound of the motor and stop in time to change batteries; but even so, your shot may have been ruined.

It's wise to include an auxiliary power supply if you plan to be doing a great deal of shooting. The auxiliary supply will greatly extend the interval between battery changes, preventing lost time for changing power cells. In cold-weather shooting, having the auxiliary power supply close to your body will keep the cells warm and their power up to snuff. Some of the time though, I find it convenient to tape the auxiliary power supply to the camera body itself. That prevents clumsy cables from tying you to your camera.

Most super 8 sound cameras, and many silent cameras, run on six AA 1.5-volt penlight cells, giving a total of 9 volts for camera systems since they are hooked up in series. It's very important to use the best-quality alkaline cells. Don't scrimp here with flashlight batteries or cells meant for flash photography: They have different characteristics.

Some manufacturers, like Kodak, offer a rechargeable power pack made up of nickel cadmium cells. These are hooked up to a charger and generally are ready to use after eight to twelve hours if fully exhausted. Other manufacturers offer battery boxes or cases which accept the usual complement of six AA alkaline cells or more powerful C cells.

There's very little to making your own auxiliary power supply. At local electronics suppliers, for under $2.00, you'll find a six-cell container that hooks up your cells in series. These battery boxes use a connector frequently found in transistor radios that use 9-volt batteries. Make sure you leave the store with one of these connectors and a connector that can plug into your camera body. Bring your camera along if there are any questions. (Most cameras use a small mini connector.)

Solder the male mini to the wire connecting to the battery container plug and you've completed your power pack. Make sure you wrap a sturdy rubber band around the pack (you can use tape) to prevent cells from loosening or falling out.

I generally use an eight-compartment box with one of the compartments shorted with a short length of wire. This in effect gives me a seven-compartment box, which I fill with nickel cadmium AA cells. They are rated at 1.3 volts each, and in series they give 9.1 volts (7×1.3). I regularly recharge these cells, and that cuts down on my battery costs.

I've stopped using nicads in the camera itself. At 1.3 volts each, they yield a voltage of only 7.8 volts (6×1.3), which may be inadequate for your power-hungry camera's needs. Now I use alkaline cells, the kind you can find in any camera shop.

Without an auxiliary power supply, I've had single-system cam-

Author's auxiliary power pack: an eight-cell holder with one of the compartments shorted out, so that the box holds seven cells. Easy to make yourself.

eras of various manufacturers deliver three to fifteen—and if you're lucky, even more—cartridges of film per set of batteries. With an auxiliary power supply, I have found the internal cell's life is greatly extended. The specific camera I am using now went through about 30 cartridges this way. Then the batteries checked a little low, so I changed them to be sure, but they probably would have given quite a few more cartridges of service when used in conjunction with an auxiliary power supply.

The auxiliary supply is usually wired in parallel with the internal supply, increasing the current available to run your camera's systems. What results is a marked reduction in how much each cell must work, significantly extending individual cell life and providing more dependable operation if there should be any greater than usual instantaneous power demands (like turning on your zoom motor).

I've come to doubt the built-in battery checks found in all cameras. Adequate up to a point, they simply don't give information about the state of the individual cells in the battery (a battery is a collection of power cells). I suggest you invest in an inexpensive battery checking meter. Such a meter can reliably tell you how good your cells really are. The built-in meter in the camera probably won't be able to distinguish between conditions like very good or only fair, and you don't want to start shooting with cells that are only so-so, risking the possibility of having them fail midway through a cartridge.

It's difficult to tell about the state of a nicad's charge, since it retains full voltage until power falls off quite suddenly. Alkaline cells, on the other hand, give plenty of warning about their ability to drive film through a camera, since their voltage, which is measured by the battery checker, falls off more gradually. And you can't use the usual voltage-ohmmeter (VOM) to check cell strength, because these units don't put a load on the cell.

You ought to be able to find a good battery checking meter for less than $15 if you shop around. Making sure it gives the same results as a bigger, more expensive unit is only common sense, so have the people in the store check it against their more expensive units.

Many super 8 single-system sound cameras use a separate 9-volt battery to power the amplifier circuitry. That battery usually lasts a long time, but you can also check it with your battery tester. Make sure you carry a spare battery.

Before I head out the door to do some shooting, I make sure I have checked my individual cells and they're at full strength. I always carry extra cells, and the battery checker to boot. You never know when one bum cell can spoil an ensemble of cells.

A Comparison of Super 8 and Videotape

When I was a boy, I read science fiction like Robert A. Heinlein's *Rocketship Galileo*, with its description of a trip to the moon. At that time, my parents and relatives thought a trip to the moon a fantastic, fanciful, unfeasible fiction. But now, so many years after watching Neil Armstrong bounce around on the moon, who has the courage to declare anything impossible?

We live in an age in which people are agog over progress and electronics. This suspension of technological disbelief can develop into an utterly foolish and hopeless faith in something called *progress,* an idea that has become an institution in the last two centuries. Just because electronic images are a newer technology than silver photography, otherwise intelligent people get carried away by the fantasy of videotape and overvalue its potential. Mention movie making, and many people conjure up a hand-cranked camera and a flickering, silent screen.

Yesterday, for example, a psychiatrist asked me if there were some way super 8 sound movies could be made with cartridges that run longer than the 50-footer (three minutes and twenty seconds at the standard 18-fps rate). He told me that at one of the large camera shops downtown a salesperson assured him that nothing larger than the 50-foot sound cartridge was available.

The psychiatrist had been on the verge of buying a Sony Portapak black-and-white camera-recorder, a videotape outfit that would set him back between $1,500 and $2,000, but which can run 30 minutes or longer without changing tapes. After talking to me, he will probably buy either a Kodak Supermatic 200 ($465 list) or the new Sankyo XL-200S ($665 list), both XL (existing light) sound-on-film, machines that will accept Eastman's 200-foot cartridge, which runs 13½ minutes.

The only further equipment he'll need for a functioning sync-sound outfit is a sound projector whose list price can range anywhere from $200 to $2,000. Complete, this amounts to a savings of one-third to a half of the roughly equivalent VTR (videotape-recorder) outfit. The shrink is planning to use super 8 for recording disturbed or actually psychotic children and their parents. As I understand his intention, parents and children are to be filmed interacting together, and the unedited footage shown to the parents during the course of their children's treatment; this will, in effect, be a new basis for the participants to observe their personal relationships.

He has already tried a VTR and had difficulty with its operation. For most people, operating both a VTR camera and a recorder is a complicated task. Complaints usually concern recurring equipment breakdown and the difficulty of operation and editing. Using a super 8 sound-on-film camera is a snap. What the doctor felt he needed most in a visual medium were color and the ability to record moving images in ordinary room light. With the usual black-and-white VTR systems, at least 40 foot-candles of incident light is required for a satisfactory image. Super 8's XL color cinematography requires a mere 5 foot-candles—what a 100-watt bulb will give off at 10 feet—making shooting in just about any light practical. With regard to color, VTR users have even a shorter stick: the lowest-cost color video cameras retail around $1,500, and that's above and beyond the price of the VTR itself. This boosts an initial video investment to $3,500 compared to as low as a few hundred dollars for super 8 equipment.

What the psychiatrist needed was a sharp color image that could be taken in existing light and then viewed on a screen measured in feet, not inches. It's a simple matter to project super

8 on a 5-foot screen with any one of a number of quality projectors. Moreover, with a super 8 videoplayer like the $1,700 VP-1 by Eastman, super 8 can be displayed electronically on any TV set. In terms of conversion, it is a simple operation to make a high-quality transfer of color film to tape in the ½-inch or cassette formats, while it is expensive to transfer tape into film.

Things look even rosier for super 8 if we include editing in the cost analysis. Video requires two or more recorders for electronic, hands-off editing. Unlike film, tape cannot be cut physically. So with two recorders, the editing hardware for a black-and-white setup runs about $4,000, while an Elmo or Bolex or EPOI viewer with mag head sound reader lists about $140 or a Goko or Elmo motorized viewer at about $300. A Super8 Sound motorized editing bench comes in at around $900, while a deluxe editing machine, an MKM horizontal editing table, is about $2,500.

Since we've already covered in depth the cost of "hardware," as people into video jargon like to call it, let's get to that vital question of software: tape or film stock and processing. Video is the outfront winner in terms of production costs if software, and software alone, is all that's considered. Shooting half an hour in the popular ½-inch format costs about $15 a roll, coming to about 50 cents a minute for black-and-white and color. Super 8 color sound-on-film in the Ektasound 50-foot cartridge is about $3.00 a minute, processing included (cost estimates based on generally available discount prices). So ½-inch tape, requiring no processing, comes to about one-sixth the price of super 8 sound filming.

I haven't said a word yet about the reusability of tape, a factor exceedingly difficult to include neatly in calculations. Although it's always an option, the benefit of reusage may be no advantage at all since many users simply do not erase and reuse what they have shot.

So what's our final cost analysis? VTR hardware breaks down this way: black-and-white camera $500, color camera $1,500, VTR $1,500, TV receiver $400 to $600, two tape decks for editing $2,000 to $4,000 each. That might be getting to be $10,000 already. If you want to get by for less, there's always the pooling of equipment, with all the hassles and inconvenience that implies. And it's my impression that people into video have to be equipment freaks to keep up with the breakdowns and mishaps.

Filmmaking hardware is comparatively reliable. For a similar super 8 setup of camera, editing equipment, and projector, the range is from a minimum of a few hundred dollars up to a couple of thousand for a first-rate system. And dollars saved for super 8 hardware can be applied to film and processing.

Like the psychiatrist, many people will be turning to super 8 who just a year or so ago would have instantly, and justifiably, turned to video to solve their problems. Unless instant playback is an absolute requirement or you genuinely prefer the creamy, relatively low-definition video image to the crisp rendition of film, super 8 remains the choice for many purposes, especially if simplicity of operation, reliability, easy editing, low-light capability, and large-screen projection are important factors.

My acquaintance the psychiatrist posed his question several years ago, so this comparison was made in the context of the then prevalent reel-to-reel, half inch wide VTR format. Today a similar comparison should be made with regard to the Beta and JVC cassette formats. Most of these popular consumer items come in the form of decks that cost in the $1,000 range and that need AC power, since they were meant to be used in conjunction with a TV set.

But we're really interested in the portable versions of these decks, which are just appearing, and these are going to be in the $1,500 price range. Progress has been made in color camera design, and there are some designs under $1,000, but these still need ten times as much light as an XL camera. Although the day may be coming when technical VTR snags are worked out, and hardware costs are lower, that day hasn't arrived, and the comparison I've outlined remains essentially valid.

Is It True What They Say About Kodachrome?

It's difficult to conceive of super 8 without Kodachrome film. Kodachrome, with a good camera and projector, shows off the medium at its best. Traditionally, a good-quality photographic image is one that has fine grain, good sharpness, accurate or pleasing colors, a balanced scale of light to dark tonal gradation, and pleasing contrast.

With the new Kodachrome 40 (K40), we are witnessing the third major change in Kodachrome film since its introduction in 1935. In that year, the relatively stark and high-contrast Kodachrome made its appearance in the 16mm format. Then almost three decades later, Kodachrome of radically different appearance, called Kodachrome II (KII), was introduced. It had less contrast, finer grain, far more pleasing color, and was sharper than its forerunner. How does the newest Kodachrome product compare? Before I can answer this question, let me explain my past experience with KII.

My deep interest in filmmaking more or less coincided with the introduction of the super 8 system in 1965. A year or two earlier, I had used KII while shooting in standard 8mm. And I have been using Kodachrome more or less regularly since that time. I've used it for 16mm films, when the professional motion picture labs advised against it, and I have been happy with the results. In fact, with the introduction of the new low-contrast print stocks that allow you to make good prints from the original camera film, it's gotten easier to use Kodachrome for both 16mm and 8mm. Prior to the introduction of materials like Ektachrome 7399 or Gevachrome 9.03 print film, prints made from KII looked very contrasty, and were a far cry from anybody's idea of good pictorial quality.

Kodachrome KII itself was a luscious film. It could capture finely detailed textures and had very accurate color representation. Of course, any appraisal of color film is ultimately subjective. In terms of scientific tests, all color films are inaccurate. Practically speaking, it isn't possible to represent accurately all the colors of the spectrum when using only three dyes (magenta, cyan, and yellow). So when I speak of Kodachrome's "accurate" color representation, I really mean that it has pleasing colors which look like they are accurate.

Kodachrome KII color rendition could run from brilliantly saturated colors to very subtle effects. But its superiority was based almost equally on two other qualities as important as pleasing color: grain and sharpness. Kodachrome had very fine grain, most clearly perceived in the color of the sky. It also had a terrific capacity for storing fine detail. Actually, it's remarkable that the tiny super 8 frame could contain such a wealth of information, seemingly about every leaf on a tree and every blade of grass in a field. The effect created of a myriad elements, of texture and detail, is one of the most enjoyable aspects of photography.

So after years of using the film, I got to know it. I got to like it, which is a mild understatement. So I'll admit it. I loved Kodachrome II. At last, I've gotten it off my chest. I loved you Kodachrome II! And what happened? You got bumped off by those guys in Rochester!

According to Eastman Kodak, replacement was necessary for several reasons. First, Kodachrome is also a popular material for shooting slides or transparencies, so the needs of still photographers had to be taken into account. Second, the new Kodachrome film is more ecologically sound. It requires fewer processing steps and uses less troublesome chemicals, which adds up to less pollution from chemical solutions carried off in waste water. You see, we are dealing not simply with a new film, but a new process which is incompatible with the old process.

So what about this new Kodachrome 40? How does it compare? First of all, let me say that the new film is the same speed as the old. Both have an EI of 40 without the 85 filter for tungsten light and an EI of 25 with the 85 filter for daylight. It's easy to compare two super 8 films. Shoot a few feet of your subject, pop out the KII cartridge, and pop in the K40 cartridge. I did this with a variety of test and real-life subjects, including color charts, gray scales, grass, sky, people, lemons on a neighbor's trees, my kid's toys (which come in many colors), and a day at the beach.

Shooting a standard color chart and a Kodak gray scale, I learned that the density and color purity of both films were remarkably accurate. To my eyes, both KII and K40 had only the slightest trace of a cyan stain. And the major difference in their color was that the new film had a more accurate yellow. The discontinued film produced an inaccurate lemony yellow, which is fine if you want to shoot lemons. In both cases blue was very good, but the K40 blue was decidedly more vibrant, with skies filming somewhat bluer.

The magenta story was like that of cyan. Both had good magenta, but the K40 magenta seemed to me to be more accurate and more vibrant. The reds of both films had too much orange, and greens for both were quite muddy; but in these areas K40 showed a little bit of improvement over KII. In both cases the pure cyan appeared to be too blue. But there was slightly more differentiation between blue and cyan in my filmed K40 chart than in my filmed KII chart.

I want to stress that the differences were moderate. In fact, it occurred to me that they were so subtle, I could almost have been looking at two different emulsion batches of the same film.

But if you think that you can tell exactly how a film will perform in the real world by shooting a test chart, you are in for a minor jolt. The pigments used for test charts are, after all, just particular pigments. What we call green can be produced by technology and nature in a variety of ways. If the test chart indicated that greens would be muddy, it related information about one, mechanically made green pigment, not all the varieties of leaves and grass. For example, the new Kodachrome does a splendid job on reporting these natural colors, but only a second-rate job of reporting the green paint on my patio floor. My patio floor is a dark green, but the new Kodachrome sees it as a muddy green.

The new film may be a margin less grainy than the old film. I compared the graininess by shooting sky until I was blue in the face, and it's damn hard to see that much of a difference between the two films. Kodachrome 40 has slightly less contrast than the old film, and it has more exposure latitude. Its ability to handle a shot with subjects in both deep shade and sunlight was impressive.

So Kodachrome 40, I love you too, but I don't know if you'll meet all my filming needs either. Kodak recently introduced a new slide film called Kodachrome 64 (K64). It's about 2½ times faster than the K40; it has higher contrast, fine grain, and it's sharp. According to Kodak, K64 won't be available in super 8, though we could use it for those light-hungry super 8 cameras with 8:1 or 12:1 zoom lenses and light-gulping finders and meters.

I have found that I cannot take pictures in dark, stormy weather or in deep shade with my $850 super 8 camera when it's loaded with K40. At times like these, I wish I had K64. So how about it, Kodak?

The 200-Foot Cameras—
For Four Times the Fun!

I've been waiting for the Sankyo XL61-200S for several years now. Not that I've not done other things to pass the time but in 1973, when Kodak introduced the 50-foot Ektasound cartridge and cameras, they also said a 200-foot cartridge was on the way. Shortly after the 50-foot products appeared, sound cameras accepting these cartridges were offered by other maufacturers, Sankyo amongst them. The Sankyo cameras looked like they were ready to accept a bigger cartridge with just a simple modification to the loading door. In fact, that's what people at Sankyo thought. One of them even said so when he rushed past me at Brooks, a camera shop in San Francisco.

So fool that I am, I ran this information way back in *The Super 8 Book,* and in the pages of *Super 8 Filmaker,* and readers have been nagging me about the Sankyo 200-foot cartridge camera for almost four years. In 1975, Eastman finally introduced the Supermatic 200 camera, with its 200-foot cartridge accepting either fast Ektachrome 7242 or 7244 in those big black plastic boxes. But filmmakers were still not satisfied.

Kodak's Supermatic 200 is a so-so camera. It runs very noisily and there is some electronic crackling in the sound track, especially at the head of each shot. It exhibits a great deal of frame-to-frame exposure variation, resulting in a sometimes flickering image, while the servo drive system hunts for the proper fps rate.

Sankyo XL61-200S shown with 200-foot cartridge in place.

Having all but condemned the camera, let me say that this non-reflex unsophisticated machine with a limited zoom ratio $f/1.2$, 9 to 21mm lens is capable of turning out good sync-sound movies more often than not, and I've got the footage to prove it. One simply has to live with its defects and make the appropriate compensations in shooting techniques. All in all, the $465 list (don't forget how much photographic merchandise is discounted) is really rather modest.

But what filmmakers still wanted was a more interesting camera —the kind Sankyo once seemed to be promising. Then, in 1978, the 200-foot cartridge-accepting Sankyo XL61-200S, based on the 50-foot-accepting Sankyo XL-600S, was introduced. And it has that long-awaited hinged flap in the top of the loading door to accommodate the top of the 200-foot cartridge. (It accepts the 50-foot cartridges internally.) It has a number of inner changes as well, the most significant being that the motor can develop about 50 percent more torque needed to drive all that extra film at a nice steady rate. All the features of the original XL-600S are preserved: the $f/1.2$, 7.5 to 45mm lens which stops down to $f/45$ and focuses right up to the front element at the 7.5mm setting, the 200-degree XL shutter, the exceptionally bright and contrasty viewfinder loaded with useful readout, the manual and automatic sound level and diaphragm controls, and the sound-picture fader. (The manual sound level control needs a VU meter to be truly useful. The level cannot be set accurately with the monitor circuit and phones.) The power zoom clutches off the motor and is operable only when the camera is running at its 18 or 24 fps rates. The grip holds six AA cells.

All of this sounds like par-for-the-course for the great number of super 8 single-system cameras being turned out these days, primarily in factories in Japan. However, the Sankyo XL61-200S's controls are unusually well thought out, and the camera is easy to operate, in particular the trigger control (marked OFF, ON, R-L). In the ON position, the camera will stop when pressure is removed from the trigger, while in the RUN-LOCK position, it will stop after pressure is applied a second time. In most cameras, the lock button must be actuated in a separate operation, which I've found to be awkward.

In terms of mechanical noise, the machine is somewhat louder than the cream of the crop, though quieter than the Kodak 200. But then, super 8 sound cameras have gotten less noisy, so engineers have obviously learned something from several years of experience. The noise level on this one, however, while more or less acceptable at 18 fps, is more annoying at 24, and even louder with the 200-foot cartridge than the 50. This statement needs to be qualified with all sorts of ifs and buts about room acoustics and miking and so forth. Moreover, these comments are based on evaluation of a preproduction sample I've borrowed from Sankyo to make my deadline for this book. This is the most serious flaw in an otherwise honest-to-goodness jewel of a camera. The Sankyo XL61-200S lists at $665, or some $115 more than the XL-600S on which it is based.

While I'm on the subject of price, I might as well add that 7242 or 7244 Ektachrome film in four 50-foot cartridges lists at $20.84, or $1.50 more than the $19.38 list for a single 200-footer. In addition, a comparison of processing costs at the lab I use adds up to a $2.20 saving on the same amount of film. I consider $3.70 a considerable saving, and this factor alone would incline me to use the longer carts.

Evaluation of the test footage showed that the camera had no trouble driving film in the 200-foot cartridge. The pitch of voices recorded at the head and tail of the cartridge, both at 18 and 24 fps, remained constant. The camera I tested was right on the button at 18 fps, but a shade fast at 24 fps. Generally, the recorded sound was exceedingly clear and clean, and there was no wow or flutter of voices. Recordings were more brilliant at 24 than at 18 fps, but the treble control of my Eumig 824 projector could compensate for the difference. In terms of voice quality, there was actually little difference between the two speeds.

Tests were conducted with the internal set of AA cells only. No auxiliary battery was used. The longest take I made was over three minutes, and the internal power supply had no trouble driving the film. However, if you are going to do a lot of shooting, use an auxiliary power supply like the one described in "Power to Spare."

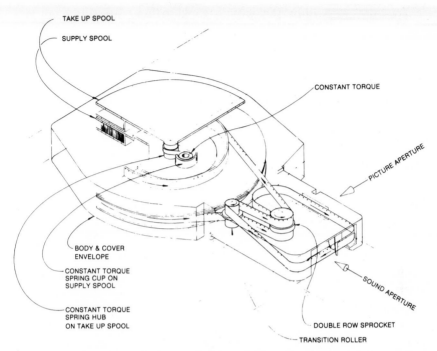

Guts of a 200-foot cartridge. Windowshade-style springs help tension spools for the even movement of the film through the device.

Camera running noise could be heard in the majority of shots, which were all miked close to the subject using a cardioid Sennheiser MD421 (a directional microphone). The camera was often kept about 5 feet from the subjects, and shots were made indoors and outdoors with the auto volume control at the HIGH position. The recorded camera noise was usually fairly low, and subsequently masked, more or less, by projector running noise.

The $f/1.2$, 7.5 to 45mm lens performed exceedingly well, even wide opened. This is a very, very good and contrasty optic. The meter system was accurate, and I did most of my shooting manually, setting the diaphragm after taking through-the-lens readings. I'd estimate that the lens wide opened was to within half a stop of the standard set by Kodak XL cameras.

You may be wondering why it took so long for this camera to appear. Several reasons have been advanced. One is that Kodak changed the specs of the 200-foot cartridge. Given such a situation, the designers were disinclined to do their thing until the cartridge was set and standardized. Another idea advanced was the absence of Kodachrome in 200-foot cartridges. But K40 is now offered in 200-foot cartridges.

I happen to think that many home moviemakers, given the choice, will opt for the longer runs. After all, a shade over 13 minutes at 18 fps (or 10 minutes at 24 fps) cuts out much of the curse of having to change cartridges in the middle of action.

We've had to wait about five years for the introduction of a sophisticated super 8 sound camera with longer loads, and this has greatly impeded the usefulness of this medium. But there's no point in watching the hole instead of the doughnut. Machines with similar quality and capability in the 16mm format cost $10,000 or more! The implications of this camera—and similar machines by other manufacturers—for the audio-visual field, for the documentarian, for TV news, and last but not least, for the creative independent filmmaker are hard to exaggerate. The formidable product ought to make a number of people take a long hard look at their commitment to video systems. Once the usefulness of the longer load hits home to most moviemakers, 50-foot-capacity cameras may become difficult to market.

At the very instant I finished writing this report, I learned that Sankyo had actually been beaten to the market place itself by Elmo, who got their 200-foot cartridge-accepting cameras into shops early in February 1978. If anybody is interested in the results of a race which has been running for several years, Sankyo was nosed out by Elmo by one month. But people in the photographic press learned about Sankyo first because of the efficient efforts of their public relations people.

The Elmo models, the 1012S-XL and the 612S-XL, are very similar except for the broader 10-1 zoom range of the 1012S, starting at 7.5mm wide and 75mm long. The lens is $f/1.2$ only at the shorter end, becoming slower as the longer focal lengths are used until it's $f/1.8$ at 75mm. This has become standard practice amongst

Elmo 1012S-XL, also shown with 200-foot cartridge in place, beat Sankyo to the marketplace.

16mm zoom lenses, since slower performance at the longer focal lengths leads to more compact designs. It's an acceptable trade-off.

Both cameras run at 18 and 24 fps, and I suspect that future 200-foot cameras will also run at both speeds for sound recording. (Some 50-foot cameras run only 18 fps.) The 1012S I examined ran very quietly, and its $1,070 list price may reflect engineering efforts in this direction.

The Elmo 1012S-XL I borrowed for testing worked splendidly, producing some of the sharpest XL images I have ever seen with some of the best recorded sound I've heard from a super 8 sound camera. Even music recordings at 18 fps had first-rate sound!

The camera is fairly well designed, with a neat-folding pistol grip that allows the machine to be properly tripod mounted. But the auxiliary and earphone inputs are placed too close to the eyepiece, and my nose bumped into connectors added to these inputs.

Actually this was the second 1012S-XL I tested. The first had a miscalibrated lens, maybe the result of having been dropped before it got to me. Images were always out of focus. I go out of my way to mention this because about a third of the cameras I receive for testing are defective right out of the box, for one reason or another.

Shooting with the camera-mounted mike, it was hard to hear the camera's mechanical noise on screening, despite the fact that the Elmo doesn't run any quieter than a number of similar good machines. It follows a pattern of mechanical noise I expect all 200-foot cameras to emulate: it's noisier at 24 fps than at 18 fps (which is true for all cameras, even 50-foot models), and it is noisier with the 200-foot cartridge than with the 50-foot cartridge. The worst possible combination is shooting at 24 fps with a 200-foot cartridge.

Short Ends I

Ektachrome, Old and New

A lot of super 8 filmmakers have the ECO blues. ECO, otherwise known as Ektachrome Commercial, or 7252, is a camera film available only in 16mm. It's rated at a hair slower than Kodachrome, but practically speaking, there's no difference. My 16mm tests show that you can get good results at double its 25 tungsten/16 daylight rating without forced processing.

My subjective appraisal of prints made from ECO original and Kodachrome original is that Kodachrome, in this case, has much finer grain. Eastman's published figures suggest that the films have similar grain, but whatever the numbers (10 root mean square (10 rms) granularity for both), Kodachrome looks less grainy. However, ECO does produce far nicer prints of most subjects.

When it was in the planning stages several years ago, Eastman had intended to rate ECO at double the speed of the film it replaced, 7255. Despite their best efforts, however, they simply could not manufacture the film at the desired speed. Moreover, the film appeared to be grainier than they had anticipated. In recent years, ECO grain has been reduced in a rather interesting manner: The film's speed has been increased so that thinner originals would be produced when shot at the given exposure index.

Many super 8 filmmakers are grief-stricken because Kodak will not put ECO in the little black cartridge we all know so well. I think we will eventually have a film like ECO to shoot, but I'll bet we have to wait for the next major improvement in the emulsion.

79

That may be just as well, since I suspect many of you would be disappointed with ECO results. I think prints made from it will prove to be too grainy for super 8.

Pressure Pad Myth

Time and again, in print and during conversation, I hear the following: Super 8 cartridges, with internal plastic pressure pads, cannot possibly produce movies that are as sharp or steady as film shot in cameras with built-in pressure pads. Now it's fine to have a concept like this one, a working hypothesis which becomes the basis for actual testing and observation. But I believe that people keep making the statement without actually checking it out. What seems reasonable and what is actually the case can be two different things.

Tests on top-of-the-line cameras with built-in pressure pads, like the Fujica ZM800, did produce sharp and steady images. But the images weren't any sharper or steadier than those produced by many good super 8 cameras using the Kodak cartridge with its own pressure pad. I suspect that people who worry about that plastic pressure pad are technological paranoids.

Super 8 cameras and projectors do a good job of registering each frame so that there's little image weave from side to side or jump up and down on the screen. With few exceptions, super 8 equipment follows the super 8 standard claw position. The equipment uses a pushdown claw that engages each perf two frames above the aperture and leaves one frame above the aperture. Since both camera and projector use the same perf for pushdown, any errors in positioning are effectively cancelled out. The now obsolete regular 8 equipment did not have such an accepted standard.

However, some super 8 cameras do have a minor but troublesome flaw: They produce *breathing* frames—fluttery, unsteady, or perhaps even out of focus—generally at the head of a shot near the tail of a silent cartridge. Usually, it's just one or two afflicted frames. Some of the better super 8 machines are more likely to produce these flaws than the box types, and I've personally had this trouble with Nizos and Beaulieus. It's interesting that I've not observed this trouble with sound cartridges.

Some people take advantage of the limited backwind facility of many super 8 cameras to perform the usual registration test of double exposing a crossed target. This test has the virtue of ruling out any registration component of the projector, since the viewer can concentrate on the relative motion of the crosses. A steady, intermittent mechanism will produce very little motion between the crosses. This, however, is not the best test for registration, for a very good reason: the super 8 backwind capability works by stuffing several feet of film into the cartridge feed chamber. When the film is exposed the second time, it does not have the usual back tension supplied by the antibackwind ratchet. Although exposures made like this can suffice for dissolves, this procedure is not adequate for registration testing. No matter how good your results may look using this testing procedure, the camera probably can do much better with properly tensioned film.

Sail from France

French inventor and camera designer Jean-Pierre Beauviala sent me a letter with details of his SAIL sound system as applied to super 8. Beauviala has perfected a method for recording sound at the film gate area of the camera and playing it back at the gate area of the projector. As you know, the sound recording head in super 8 cameras and projectors is placed a full 18 frames (or one second at 18 fps) behind the film gate aperture where the picture is being exposed. In the SAIL system, the soundhead is located within a frame or two of the aperture, and sound is recorded almost immediately adjacent to the corresponding frame. This would eliminate the gap between image and sound, vastly simplifying single-system (sound-on-film) editing. Beauviala's organization, Aäton of Grenoble, originally applied the concept to their Aäton 16mm documentary camera, but 16mm workers have shown very little interest in this innovation.

Very simply, here's how the super 8 system works: A tachometer measures the speed of the film as it goes through the gate. Remember, the film here is being advanced intermittently, one frame at a time, so the speed is not constant. To compensate for the varying speed of the film, digital electronics process the audio signal to instantaneously raise and lower the frequency for recording that will match the actual film speed at a given instant. If the resulting single-system film is played back on a vertical or horizontal editing table, the soundhead can be mounted right at the gate of the viewer. The editor can then see and hear, in sync, movies which can be cut with ease right at the frame.

Beauviala plans an adapted form of SAIL that could be used with present super 8 single-system cameras. With it you could place the soundhead on your editor-viewer at the film gate, but you would need a displacement recorder to move the sound ahead to the standard image-sound separation (18 frames) in order to prepare it for playback on a conventional projector. During filming, the

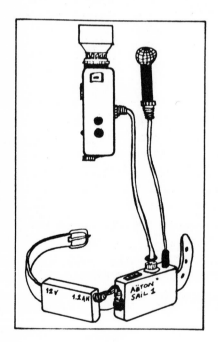

SAIL system: Mike plugs into Sail 1 unit, which uses digital memory to store sound for one second. Powered by a 12-volt battery, SAIL sends sound signal to the single-system camera's input. The result is sound recorded immediately adjacent to the image without the usual 18-frame disparity of sound compared to picture.

Aäton SAIL 1 unit, powered by a long-lived 12-volt battery, would delay the sound recorded by the camera head by one second, so that image and sound would correspond; there would be no 18-frame delay.

The SAIL system will probably be of most interest to TV station filmmakers and others in a big hurry to edit film and screen it. For TV applications, it seems to me that it would be a relatively simple matter to place a playback head right at the gate area of the Kodak videoplayer, since its film drive is continuous. In this way, super 8 TV news footage shot with the SAIL system could be sent out on the air without having to be processed by a displacement recorder that would separate sound and image by 18 frames. I've learned there have been recent cost reductions in the basic circuit component of the Sail system—the "bucket brigade"—making it possible for the unit to become a consumer product.

PC or Erlson?

Some super 8 cameras are equipped with a built-in switch that opens and closes once per frame. By interrupting a low voltage supplied by a sync recorder, the switch (like the points of an automotive distributor) provides a reference signal which keeps the recorder in sync with the camera. Unfortunately, the prestigious Beaulieu cameras don't have such a built-in switch, but they do offer an added-on accessory, the Erlson switch.

If you're about to buy an Erlson contact switch for your Beaulieu 4008, think again. I strongly recommend the PC adaptation offered by Cinema Sync Systems (14261 Avenue Mendocino, Irvine, California 92714). They charge $85 to add the PC socket, and it costs much less than the Erlson switch. Exactly how much less is a matter for you to investigate, since Beaulieu prices seem to be changing from moment to moment. The Cinema Sync conversion, unlike the Erlson, doesn't get in the way of the main function control. Moreover, my tests show that the 4008 runs much more smoothly and draws less power using the PC, offering better operation for cable or crystal sync.

The wave of the future: automatic-focusing cameras, namely the Sankyo ES-44XL VAF. The machine uses electronics, patented by Honeywell, similar to that employed in split-image rangefinders, to measure contrast of image segments and focus the lens according to voltage outputs. Although Elmo has shown a prototype of a similar machine, this silent unit from Sankyo is the first on the market.

The Bolex 551 XL Sound Camera

When the first super 8 single-system cameras, the Kodak Ekta-sound cameras, appeared in 1973, they made a terrible racket. The trouble was that they were just as loud as run-of-the-mill silent cameras. But a sound camera has to run very quietly indeed, in order not to make itself heard on the recording.

The professional motion picture industry has established standards of performance for format camera's running noise, and there are established testing methods. The camera is usually placed in a special acoustical chamber lined with sound-deadening material. If you've ever been in one of these rooms, you know about the weird sensation that makes you feel as if your ears are plugged.

Located 3 feet from a tripod-mounted camera is a microphone that is plugged into electronics displaying the sound level on a meter that registers the intensity on a decibel (dB) scale. Acceptable performance is usually considered to be about 28 to 30dB, and a machine in this range will be usable on a sound stage, where the requirements are especially rigorous. Usually, sync-sound filming in the field or for documentary work is a little more relaxed.

There are very quiet cameras, but there are no noiseless cameras. If you hold a microphone a foot or less from the camera, you'll probably pick up its running noise loud and clear. If you tried this with a cassette or reel-to-reel tape recorder of even moderate quality, chances are you'd have a hard time picking up any running noise.

There is no super 8 camera that meets the standards I've discussed here. The 35 and 16mm Mitchells and Arris and Eclairs meant for sync-sound work are far quieter than anything super 8 filmmakers have at their disposal. But the running noise levels of super 8 cameras have been steadily dropping. For example, second-generation Ektasound cameras from Kodak are quieter than the first. And second-generation sound cameras made in the Chinon factory are a whisper of what they were.

The Chinon factory makes the 551 XL sound camera for Bolex, and it purrs along at a rather respectably low level. I can't rate it

Bolex 551XL.

on the decibel scale; I don't have the equipment, and chances are the rating would be discouraging when compared with the figures you'd get from testing a CP-16. But the Bolex 551, and similar cameras from Elmo and Nizo, makes me think that it would be a good idea for super 8 manufacturers to investigate a way to apply the same standards to their equipment.

I've been working with the 551 for a short time now, and although the focus of this rap is its low sound level, it is a highly respectable super 8 sync-sound camera with a high-quality $f/1.2$, 8 to 40mm lens. The recorded sound is very good, too. My major complaint is that this camera, so obviously meant for filmmakers with serious aspirations, does not have a 24-fps running speed. It

runs at 18 fps and takes still frames and has a built-in intervalometer, but the important 24 fps—for people who may need to blow
up the film to 16mm, or for compatibility with some TV film chains
—is missing.

Nevertheless, in terms of running noise, the 551 sets a standard
that most super 8 sound cameras ought to but cannot reach. There
are even a couple of machines for four or five times the list price
that are far noisier. I'm not saying that the Bolex is the end of the
line, for even here improvement is possible. I, for one, won't be
satisfied until super 8 machines are as quiet as their 16 and 35mm
counterparts. But until something better comes along, I can think
of no good reason to settle for less. With a modest list of $575 for
the quality and features of the 551, listen carefully and hear if you
might not be getting taken with a costlier machine that runs louder.

Universal Hydralock Tripod

Fluid-head tripods are often used for filmmaking in the larger
formats, but there's no reason why they can't be useful for making
super 8 movies. Until rather recently though, these heads were
scaled to the needs of larger formats, which meant they were bigger,
bulkier, and more expensive than they needed to be for super 8.

Fluid heads operate on a hydraulic principle: A fluid is forced,
under pressure, from one chamber to another, controlling the pan-
ning or tilting movement of the head. The result is exceptionally
smooth camera movement. In fact, you have to put out some
effort to make a fluid head give jerky motion. Fluid heads themselves, the upper part of the tripod, can be purchased separately,
so they are usable with a number of wooden-leg tripod models.

There are two prime choices for super 8 filmmakers (or 16mm
filmmakers with lightweight cameras like the Scoopic, Beaulieu, or
Bolex models) in the fluid-head field today: one model each from
Miller and Universal. The units are similar. Both were designed by
Robert E. Miller of Australia. The Universal head is slightly larger
and slightly less expensive (about $355 compared with $370 in a
local shop for both head and legs) than the Miller, making it a

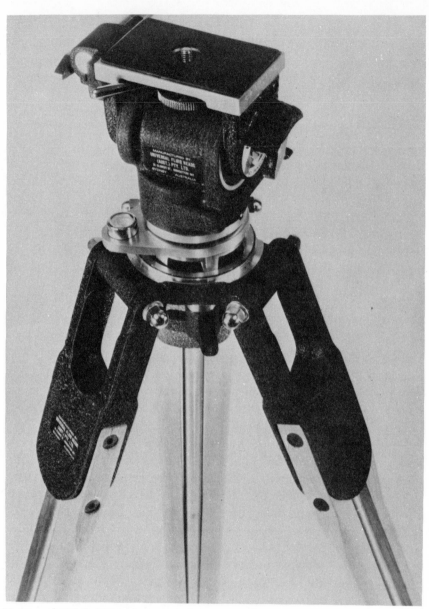

Universal 808 fluid head, mounted on a tripod.

slightly better buy. The Universal Hydralock,. which I tested, worked well enough to make me go out and buy one after 14 years of yearning.

More in keeping with the spirit of super 8 is the $50 fluid head from Bilora, which seems to work as smoothly as its more expensive counterparts. Check it out for yourself.

Section 3

Recording the Image

Introduction:

On Location with Super 8 and 16mm

The state of moving-image technology determines the form and content of films. If nobody had ever invented the 16 and 8mm film-making systems, a great deal of the richness of expression and intimacy of the film medium would be lost to us. The smaller size and economic advantages of these "miniature" formats has given filmmakers areas of expression that would have been impossible to achieve in the 35mm format used for theatrical films.

The hope of George Eastman and colleagues when they introduced 16mm in 1923 was that they were presenting the world with a motion picture system which could be used by home movie-makers in the same way that the original Kodak still cameras and film had been used to compile snapshots for the family album. But that hope did not fulfill the original dream. Sixteen millimeter was too costly for most people, and perhaps spool-loading cameras were too complex to operate. However, 16mm made unexpected inroads in an area that scarcely existed before it was introduced: the audio-visual field. One important step took place during the Second World War, when reduction prints of feature films for entertainment and instructional films made for the armed services were shown to GI's all over the world. It took more than two decades after its introduction, but 16mm finally became a respected method of film production, and not simply a medium for the distribution of films shot in the larger, theatrical format.

Eight millimeter and then the improved version, super 8, were offered to the public. Today, super 8 is being used in a number of situations where 16mm would have been impossible. The initial papers published on the format by Kodak in 1964 indicated that super 8 was meant to be an improved audio-visual medium. (Once again, the dreams of the founders were thwarted. While super 8 is used in audio-visual, it isn't nearly as big as it could have been, since 16mm has remained dominant, with a great many users favoring videotape.) But in 1965, super 8 film, housed in its quick-loading cartridge, was introduced, and all the existing spool-loading 8mm hardware was made obsolete in a single stroke. Now that we are in the second decade of super 8, it still has not reached the status of a production format. In fact, there are very few people making a living at commercial super 8 filmmaking, while there are quite a few doing quite well with 16mm and videotape.

One reason for this situation is that once professional budgets are involved—with professional salaries, travel expenses, and so forth—it becomes difficult to support arguments in favor of super 8's lower cost compared with 16mm. This will probably always be the case. Super 8's chief asset in situations like this has to be something other than reduced stock and processing costs. One could be *intimacy*. Super 8 equipment is less fearsome to most people you are likely to film than 16mm gear. Super 8 cameras, smaller and less formidable than their 16mm counterparts, are, after all, home-movie instruments, and they look like what they are.

I had originally planned to shoot my film *Revelation of the Foundation* in 16mm, but tests in super 8 convinced me that I'd get a better, more intimate portrait of my subjects with less intrusive gear. Lawrence Halprin originally planned to shoot his experiences designing the Dali museum in super 8, but increased funding caused him to change his mind, and the film, *Le Pink Grapefruit*, was shot in 16mm. Julio Neri is a Venezuelan filmmaker and organizer of the International Super 8 Film Festival which takes place each year in Caracas. His films are strong political statements that explore the history of his country, but he keeps food on the table by shooting weddings for clients.

In this section we will take a look at different ways of making films —both with super 8 and 16mm. There are, in a very real sense, as many ways to make films as there are filmmakers. May yours, as Don Juan would say, be a path with heart.

Filming Revelation of the Foundation

It looks like the dregs down by the water at Gate Five, Sausalito. Called Waldo Point by the people who live in that floating town, it is the berth of scores of houseboats—not the neat, tidy ones you'll find just a few hundred feet south along the shore of Richardson Bay. No, the Point is more like a floating shantytown, set adrift from convention and normalcy, where you make your way to the boat you seek by traversing a bobbing network of raft walkways.

But the raft walkways connect brightly decorated boats; the gulls and the Marin hills, with fog streaming through the valleys, make a backdrop that isolates Waldo Point like a movie set. It was about seven years ago that Paul Foster, former Hog Farmer and Merry Prankster who then found Jesus and is a lot happier for it, first took me to the floating home, or should I say room, of Uncle Bill. Uncle Bill ran the American Buddhist Ashram for several years at the height of the madness in the late sixties. The Ashram was in the Haight, San Francisco's transient psychedelic medina.

Uncle Bill lived for a year with a Tibetan family in Nepal, and for another year with Alan Watts who, with his family, called Bill "guru," as do many local people who are into the Eastern thing. Uncle Bill looks like an aged sage—a white-bearded wizard, venerable and wise, given to hyperbolic philosophical fancies. It's all true. Uncle Bill is an aged sage, and more.

When I first saw him, Uncle Bill was standing on his abbreviated front porch throwing bread out to the birds. The porch was a risky

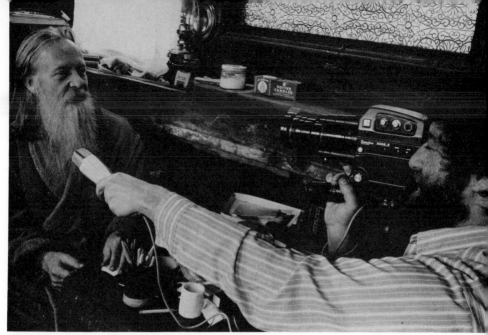

The author interviews the aged sage and white-bearded wizard, Uncle Bill (photo by Rod Wyatt, *Super 8 Filmaker*).

perch at that, since Bill has taken at least one header into the waters of Sausalito Bay—an excursion not to be recommended since the boats have no plumbing.

Soon I was visiting Uncle Bill a couple of times a week for many months. Then winter. The picturesque life on the water became less comfortable as the chill set in and survival became more important than just grooving on the surface.

Bill had an invitation to move to a house in San Francisco from a man he had befriended in the Haight days—an Indian yogi, a Bengali named Cirangiva Roy, known to his followers as "Father" and regarded by them to be either *the* deity or *a* deity. Father, it was also alleged, had many wives, and he was known for his extroverted personality expressed in his grandiloquent, flamboyant style.

On the pages of his notebook, Uncle Bill listed for the interested reader, with colored pens, two columns of qualities—his and Father's —and these turned out to be two columns of total opposites in terms of philosophy and personality. So, said Uncle Bill, I will never go and live with him, even if his house is warm.

A few days later, I returned to find Bill's floating room listing to one side more than usual because its mooring ropes were not properly adjusted. Rounding the floating pathway to the front door, I looked through the glass windows. This room always felt like a basement room, a floating basement room, maybe the only one in the world. Through the glass I saw that everything was gone, including Uncle Bill. Moreover, there were signs of a hasty departure. Remember, Charlie Manson had just been found out, and my mind was set to working double time, as you may well understand.

I had with me a Fuji single 8 camera and some black-and-white film, and I walked in and filmed the empty shelves which had been stocked with cassette recordings of Tibetan Buddhist mantras and lined with books about Eastern religion. I filmed Bill's empty seat, which looked less like a throne to me now that it had lost its plush red pillows. Where were the tonkas, those paintings from Tibetan mythology blessed with rich earth colors, reds and gold pigments? Gone, gone, gone—all gone. Set adrift along with Uncle Bill, along the pathless path.

From time to time I had taken films of Uncle Bill. The newly introduced Kodak sound-on-film super 8 cameras were ideal for setting down some of Uncle Bill's raps. I just fell into filming Bill, without forming a specific plan for a movie, but with many vague plans forming all at once.

After filming his empty floating shell, I talked to some of Uncle Bill's neighbors. I found a blond, bearded man who had seen Uncle Bill taken away, so it seemed to him, by a group of people. Yes, my informant had seen Cirangiva with them. The neighbor had seen someone in the group point a gun at Uncle Bill, and, shortly thereafter, he was spirited away in a Rolls Royce. To compound my concern, Bill's neighbor had been in Calcutta several years before at a time when Cirangiva had a large following. It was there that he had first seen the man, and he told me that Father had a decidedly unsavory reputation.

My next step was to find Malachi, a friend of Bill's who plays guitar music inspired by the religion of Tibet. Malachi had once had a large cult of followers himself, in Santa Fe. One dark day, Malachi discovered the worst kind of infidelity within his ranks. He retired to his temple to meditate upon this, when suddenly, in the middle of the summer (I am told), it began to snow, and it snowed for two days. During that terrible time in the temple, Malachi exhausted his spiritual energy, as I understand it. But to tell you the truth, I don't really understand any of it. I am just reporting the facts, facts as I know them to be. What more can you expect from me?

So I looked up Malachi, who was important for two reasons: first, he had many connections in San Francisco's convoluted Eastern religion scene, and second, he had a black belt in Karate. It was Malachi who persuaded me to see Bruce Lee in *Enter the Dragon*, and I remember filming the screen with a super 8 low-light camera the first time we went to a Kung Fu movie.

But this time, engrossed in my quest for Uncle Bill, I put aside my camera. Malachi and I finally found a person who set us on the proper path, and we went over to Scott Street, to the headquarters of the Foundation of Revelation, to the home of Father and his followers.

It was a normal-enough-looking San Francisco pseudo-Victorian house, cut up into four railroad flats, a corner house of no real pretensions or special dread. We knocked on the door, ready for the worst. After a few minutes of nervous waiting on the front steps, Uncle Bill came to the door and ushered us in. We embraced him, and then walked down a basement hallway lined with garbage cans until we came to a door made of wallboard, which swung aside to let us enter Uncle Bill's room.

Bill's room had been outfitted and furnished, or was in the process of being decorated, to resemble his former floating houseboat home. The walls were brick and the ceiling was unfinished. (In the months to come, Bill would cover the joists with egg cartons in an attempt to subdue the noise from the room above.) There was one small octagonal window, high in the side of one wall. The window was at ankle level on the street, and through it dogs would often look at us. The window bowed inward like the top of a diamond.

Yes, he had been kidnapped, Bill told us, but no, he did not want to leave. If these people needed him that much, then he ought to stay. No, it had not been a real gun, it had been a toy gun, and the kidnapping had been done in the spirit of a joke, but on the other hand, it may not have been as carefree as all that. Bill cannot answer a question directly. Just as his expression can change instantly from that of a merry elf to mercurial wizard, his answers to straight-forward questions are elliptical and convoluted. His responses leave the questioner spinning in a gush of words—a rap that tends to see all sides of the issue, or in fact, all sides of many issues only casually related to the main topic, which can tend to be forgotten.

I never really found out the exact circumstances of Bill's leaving the water for dry land, and in the spring, summer, fall, and part of the next winter, I got different versions of that day. During those 11 months, I brought my camera to film Bill more and more frequently. Some of the footage finally found its way into an assemblage of life in the Bay Area I called *Children of the Golden West*.

As we sat and talked in the basement room, we could feel the energy of the entire house—the headquarters of the Foundation of Revelation—above us. There were frequent visits from Father's followers. One woman in particular came by regularly to bring Bill tea and food from one of the kitchens above. Food was specially prepared for Uncle Bill because the cuisine served upstairs was usually spicy hot Indian food. Sheila U.S.A., as the woman was known, would visit Bill, bringing with her bland food and many words about Father and his divinity.

Sheila player the guitar and sang, and sometimes we talked about Father who was becoming more and more interesting to me. For many weeks I heard about the man, and although he visited Bill frequently, I still had never seen him. (Bill usually stayed in his room, and people came to him, not only from that particular house, but from all over, since Father's divine family is far-flung.) Sheila and the rest of Father's followers believe that he is God and that he is the creator of the universe. I later learned from Father's very lips that he makes no such claim, although he did say that God speaks directly to him. As I've said, Father remained a distant but increasingly formidable figure.

Many of Father's followers were brought by or dropped in to

see Bill, since by this time he had become an important part of the household, raised to a kind of celebrity status. They considered Bill to be Buddha—not Buddha-like or a Bodhisattva, but the Buddha himself—just as they considered Father to be Shiva, the Hindu deity. There really was no arguing with them about this, and honestly, I didn't argue with Sheila, who I came to like more and more.

Because Bill rarely left his room, I brought a projector to him and showed him footage of himself or other things I was working on—films partway completed or just footage he might find interesting. But most of the time, we simply discussed religion and philosophy and ourselves. Bill began to talk to me about the people in the house, and I met more and more of them as they entered his room, removing their shoes, then hugging Bill, and most often sitting in the lotus position on one of the cushions. If Bill left the room, I had a chance to speak to them alone, and they affirmed that Bill was indeed Buddha and that Father was God.

One day Father entered the room, and so I met a short, thin Indian gentleman with a deep voice and a rich accent who laughed most of the time. Father just twinkled and hugged people and held

Bearded Cirangiva Roy, known to his followers as "Father," at the airport, leaving for India. Author would have followed Father to India but the terms of his AFI grant specified that no funds could be spent outside of the USA (photo by Victor Hamilton).

hands. He had long hair, but he was balding, and he had a long white beard. I figured he must be about 60 years old.

The next time I saw Father, he was hobbling down the front stairs, his beard shaved off, looking like hell. He didn't recognize me as we passed. Bill told me that Father had been in an automobile accident. He had been drinking and went off the road near the family commune in Willits. Father seemed to do everything to excess, with lots of drinking, partying, and wives, and I wondered why these people considered the man a deity. Some of the followers were very intelligent, and this added to the mystery, since it is my prejudice that faith is for the simple-minded. But upon reflecting, it may well be that faith is for the simple-hearted.

The next time I met Father, he was recovered from his accident and was between trips to New York or Australia or I really don't know where (he was always in motion). At that time our president, Richard Nixon, was making headlines for himself in China, and China was the topic of conversation. Father was complaining about the United States and praising China, and I said something I had thought myself incapable of saying: I told Father that if he liked China so much, he ought to move there and see if they let him do there what he was doing here. This caused a bit of a row, with Uncle Bill telling me I had been impolite, that this was Father's house and his beliefs should be respected. So you see, Father had the ability to make ordinarily reasonable people say extraordinary things.

Several times, Father was in Bill's basement room when I was showing movies, and he liked what he saw. It was my wildest dream come true when he turned to me and said, "Lenny, you must make a movie about me." This was an invitation I could not refuse.

For years I had been thinking about what happens to people in groups, that is, communal groups, or small groups with a common purpose. People, or creatures that resemble people, have been living together in tight-knit units for two- to four-million years, and this kind of collective experience is part of our heritage. Our invention of the city has fragmented the once close group experience of humanity, and, I believe, has set us upon a self-destructive course.

I had made *Far Out, Star Route,* a documentary film showing the point of view of an insider in a commune in the Oregon countryside. I was the insider, and my friends and I experimented with this new lifestyle, which is as old as the human story. So this opportunity to study Father and the group of people who considered themselves to be his followers, or Gods and Goddesses as they called themselves (every man is a God and every woman a Goddess), was, if you'll pardon the expression, a godsend.

An overall plan for the film emerged. I decided that I would use Bill as an interlocutor, cutting from action upstairs in the house to Bill in his basement room. Although I had been talking with and observing Father and his followers, and discussing them with Bill, I simply did not understand why they followed Father. At least I could not get a gut feeling for it. But belief is based on faith, and all religious belief transcends understanding. Either you know or you don't know, and I didn't know.

I wrote a grant proposal for the film, which I called *Buddha in the Basement,* and sent it off to the American Film Institute. A few months later, the AFI said yes, and I was promised $10,000 with which to make the film. I planned to shoot in 16mm, but at that moment, I was deeply into investigating super 8 sync-sound systems for *The Super 8 Book.* Therefore, the first experiments I tried at the Foundation of Revelation were with simple super 8 sync-sound cameras. By this time Bill had moved to another basement room several miles down Castro Street in an area called Diamond Heights, on a windswept slope overlooking the city. I figured that I could continue to film him in his basement and intercut his comments with the footage shot at Scott Street, just as I had originally planned. But I never did use this approach. I discovered that I did not need an interlocutor, and that this device would only slow down or, in fact, bring the flow of the footage to a grinding halt. So, for the most part, Uncle Bill got left on the cutting room floor, something which made him very happy. So, too, the film's title had to be changed; it became *Revelation of the Foundation.*

Hari, a follower of Father and the group's filmmaker, had made a number of films about Father for showing within the group and to outsiders. The costs of these 16mm projects had been borne by

Hari, and they taxed his resources. When he saw me shooting tests with a GAF 205, he wondered about this new medium of lip-sync super 8 sound-on-film and grasped its potential, expecially after I screened some of the first rushes for him. I was impressed myself. The footage was terrifically good, and it dawned on me that this was the way to shoot the film—in super 8 and not in 16mm as I originally planned.

If I went the usual 16mm production route, I would have only enough money for maybe an hour or two (at the most) of shooting. In a verité-style film, so heavily dependent upon happenstance (or synchronicity, if you want to get metaphysical), this would probably cut to less than a half-hour film. But I wanted to do something in depth. After all, I had what I considered to be a lot of money, a fortune in fact, and as I examined my options, I came to realize that if I shot the film in 16mm, I would wind up with a superficial statement. As a result, I shot the film in super 8, at 18 fps, and wound up with a 60-minute film out of 200 cartridges, or about 10 hours of sync footage. I also recorded about 10 hours of sound with a Sony TC55 cassette recorder, and shot additional silent footage with a Beaulieu 4008 M3. I used the GAF 805 as well as the GAF 205 XL sound-on-film machines.

In December 1974, when I started to do the technical groundwork for the film, there were only a few sync sound-on-film cameras from which to choose, including a couple of models each from Kodak and GAF and one from Beaulieu. I had hoped to use the Beaulieu 5008S, but the two samples I tried left a great deal to be desired mechanically and optically (although one I later used worked perfectly well). So, I was faced with using the very simple nonreflex Kodak models or the GAF reflex machines. Happily, the GAF cameras worked well enough, and I spent much of January shooting Father and his followers.

My technique was to hold the camera with one hand and the mike with the other. The mike was held as close to the subject as possible to get the best recorded sound with the most presence and least noise of the running camera. Today there are accessory booms for mounting the mike atop the camera, but none were available then, and the one I made myself conducted too much noise to the mike. Maybe it's just as well, since one advantage of using a handheld mike is that it can be aimed at a subject who is talking while the camera pans away to get reaction shots. Since I wanted my subjects to relate directly to me, I could not use an associate to operate the microphone.

The cinema verité style of shooting is not any different from that of the theatrical cinema, where the omnipresent camera is invisible and the characters play to each other and not to the camera. My concept was to accept the fact that I was present and allow the characters to play directly to me, or to the camera, if that was their desire. The idea of the invisible camera is, I must point out once again, an agreed-upon-convention—one that is held in great repute, but one I preferred to abandon.

It should also be pointed out that a film like this, which attempts to lay bare certain intimate aspects of people's lives, requires subjects who are extroverts. Camera-shy people simply cannot co-operate with such a project. Although people are always aware that the camera is present, its continual presence wears them down or numbs the players to its existence, and in their waning awareness come the opportunities that I seek. Conversely, beautiful opportunities are also created when people play directly to the camera, as Father often did in his attempts to persuade me that his philosophy was the only correct point of view in all creation. It's a game that everybody plays: We all know we're making a movie, and all you can do is make a movie about making a movie anyway. But I feel I'm better off filming real people living their own lives than, for example, filming Warren Beatty or Dustin Hoffman in some contrived script.

Whenever I could, I shot on Kodachrome, since it's the finest-grain and sharpest material available to the super 8 worker. When fast film was required, I shot on Ektachrome 160. Although I was grateful for the rapid-loading cartridge, its 50-foot capacity was exasperating. If I were filming now, I would have the option of shooting with the longer-running 200-foot cartridge, thus missing fewer moments while changing film.

After a rough cut down to two hours, I transferred the sound to super 8 mag film using an Elmo ST 1200 projector and the Super8

Sound recorder with a BSR graphic stereo equalizer to sweeten the sound. I cut the original, making tape splices, and after hundreds of screenings with the Elmo and repeated passes through the Super8 Sound editing bench, I didn't have a foot of scratched film until a careless moment after a year of editing (but I bet you'll never notice it).

Prints of the original were made by Leo Diner Films of San Francisco, and they are more than adequate. The first print was made on Ektachrome 7389. All subsequent prints were made on Gevachrome 9.02, which had similar low contrast but whiter whites, a blacker black, and, most important, skin colors that tended to get less ruddy or purple. The stock was striped by Kodak and they do an absolutely first-rate job of poststriping. When it comes to emulsion-side striped contact prints, I think they have no competition in terms of quality. The sound tracks for the prints were dubbed in my studio.

I've shown the film to audiences at the University of Oregon and at the California Institute of the Arts, and screenings were held at Canyon Cinematheque at the San Francisco Art Institute and at the Pacific Film Archive of the University of California. People have asked me, after the screenings, if I am one of Father's followers. I feel flattered, for the easiest kind of film to make would have been a hatchet job, condemning Father and his Divine Family. But that's not the way I feel about them. The reality is far more complex than a facile condemnation would reflect. Jesus and his disciples may well have looked this peculiar to an outsider looking in; but unlike most outsiders, I spent a year visiting my subjects before I shot a foot of film, and then shot only after their invitation to do so.

So what we have in *Revelation of the Foundation,* I believe, is a rare look at a group which may be of critical importance to the understanding of the cultural currents of our nation. It makes perfect sense to me that the gospel should be presented in the medium of film in the twentieth century, and not written, as it was 2,000 years ago.

Weddings in Super 8

Julio Neri and his wife, Mercedes, organizers of the 1977 Venezuelan Avant Garde International Super 8 Film Festival, make their living producing movies of weddings. I had a chance to accompany them on two of their assignments. One, in Caracas, was a wedding held under heavy security because the bride was a member of one of the wealthiest families in Venezuela. It was attended by a former Venezuelan president, high political officials, and, naturally enough, two presidential candidates. (Elections are held every five years and one was coming up.) The other wedding was somewhat more congenial; it took place two hours out of Caracas in the lovely town of Colonia Tovar, a community of German-Venezuelans.

Mercedes does the business end of the operation and often records sound at the weddings. The clients contact her, and she does the negotiations. The price is by the amount of film, or running time, the parents of the couple request. For a film running 350 feet of super 8 at 18 fps, Julio will shoot about eight 50-foot cartridges and charge about 2,500 bolivares, or about $600.

Lights are handled by Julio and Mercedes's friend, Andy Valencia, who handholds a single 1,000-watt quartz lamp run off the mains. Another friend works as a camera assistant, helping to change film and keep track of the cartridges. The crew gets paid a decent wage, and everybody gets to eat the wedding feast, if the voracious guests leave any food. The wedding at Tovar, which took place in the lovely near-jungle countryside hills surrounding Caracas, was a wonderful example of human gluttony that would have made

107

Venezuelan film crew: (from left to right) Andy Valencia, Julio Neri, and Chi Chou take a break.

Breughel blush. People fought with each other for first dibs at the buffet, and these chow hounds went on to beg huge portions from the overworked staff dishing out the grub. The groom, attired in a preposterously mod white tuxedo, stood near this line of guests openly gaping at their bestiality.

Enough of this. On to technical matters. Julio uses a Sankyo XL40-S single-system camera, which does a good job of recording image and sound. The film used is striped Ektachrome 160, which is processed overnight in Caracas by Kodak.

Mercedes handholds the telescoping cardioid, which is offered as a camera-mounted accessory. The mike works surprisingly well at isolating speakers from background noise, and wearing phones helps with the miking. I filled in for her awhile and found the most difficult part of the operation to be keeping the camera-connected sound cable from fouling. Especially difficult situations arise when the camera person must "cross over" from one side of the sound

Shooting wedding party against the hills of Colonia Tovar.

person to the other. Two solutions occur to me: One is to use the camera assistant to help keep the cable from snagging; the other is to use a wireless mike, like those offered by Minolta and Chinon, which transmits to a receiver mounted on the camera.

I assume that these brands could also be used in conjunction with Sankyo cameras, and there is always the option of obtaining far more costly radio mike units like those offered by Vega or Sennheiser. The major problem inherent in wireless mikes is recording spurious signals, say from CB or ham operators. The problem is probably worse in Venezuela than in the States since the local regulatory agency is reportedly lax in its enforcement.

As one might imagine, much of the wedding footage, such as the ceremony itself and afterward at the reception, is shot sync sound. Guests are in lively and extroverted frames of mind, and friends of the bride or groom are often only too willing to show themselves off as witty TV personalities. Of course the close family, such as parents and grandparents, must be filmed, and children are frequently called upon to perform.

Silent footage is shot of the food because people seem to be terribly proud of the spread, especially at Jewish weddings, Julio reports. It is also very important to get some shots of the presents, often piled high and filling an entire room.

Despite the fact that the fast $f/1.2$ Sankyo lens is capable of good performance in low light with Ektachrome 160, Neri prefers to have additional lighting to increase the snap of images. In point of fact, with the single light used, exposures are often in the $f/11$ range.

I think that Julio's wedding work would profit greatly from a cordless lamp, because the power cord is a frequent source of trouble as the place of action shifts and guests go ambling by. There are a number of portable halogen units on the market, and a unit half or a quarter as bright as the one they presently use would do the job as well. The bright lights notwithstanding, Julio and his crew, compared with the still photographers present at both weddings, are relatively unobtrusive. Most of the still photographers look like a bunch of blundering ill-at-ease oafs, while Julio gracefully blends into the event.

Editing is relatively straightforward, cutting single-system film. The portions shot silent are dubbed with music. The entire film, bereft of outtakes and with improved continuity and music, might be ready for the family in less than two weeks.

At one time Julio included a projector in the package, but he found that his unskilled clients were forever calling on him to help them operate their machines. Now he leaves the choice of projector and its purchase to the client, who can hassle it out at the store like the rest of us.

The idea of a filmmaker whose work is in what I think of as the Spanish surrealist tradition, dealing heavily with the political issues and history of his country, making a living at weddings is, to my way of thinking, no contradiction at all. Weddings too often are surrealistic events, and frequently economic or political alliances at that.

There are several filmmakers besides Julio who are shooting these affairs, and there seems to be much more super 8 wedding filmmaking going on in Caracas per capita than in the United States. It's a ripe area for young filmmakers to explore. The shooting techniques make for good practice, and there's everything right about somebody being able to make a living at what he or she does.

Filming Le Pink Grapefruit

I spent a surrealistic September 1975 in Spain, recording sound for Lawrence Halprin's Roundhouse Productions' film *Le Pink Grapefruit*. Why the fruity title? Well, it turns out that pink grapefruit is the favorite food of world-famed artist Salvador Dali, and the film is about Dali, naturally enough. It's probably the color he finds most attractive, since he also serves pink champagne at his frequent soirées. A tribute to the man's wisdom is that he himself will not drink any of this champagne.

It's easy to call him a fascist because he supported the four-decade dictatorial reign of Franco and, before the Second World War, was an admirer of Hitler. For this transgression, he was booted out of the surrealist movement. At present, he proudly characterizes himself as a monarchist, in all earnestness waiting for the return of kingdoms in Europe.

Dali has been involved with film for all of 50 years, and his association with Luis Buñuel produced the much admired film *The Andalusian Dog* (1929). Dali had a fling at Hollywood in the forties. There he contributed an intriguing dream sequence to Hitchcock's *Spellbound,* and for a time he worked with Walt Disney to create an animated film which, unfortunately, never got made.

At 73, Dali simply doesn't show his years, and he is still active in film projects. It would seem that he is continually the subject of a documentary, for while our group was in Spain, he was being filmed by Austrian TV, after which he worked on a TV commercial for a Japanese beer company.

112

Filming in Salvador Dali's garden: (from left to right) Dali, in long robe; Lawrence Halprin, director; *lips*, a Dali creation in dead-center background of photo; Paul Ryan, cinematographer holding camera, while two innocent bystanders watch. With his back to the camera is author Lipton, soundman for this project (Roundhouse Productions).

Dali's public style, which he uses before the cameras, from the look of it, must have been firmed up in the twenties. I came to think of it as Tango Style. His performance for professional film crews is not all that different from the show he puts on for the tourist with camera in hand. He thrusts his chin back and, with eyes bulging, glares directly into the lens. In these moments he resembles a refugee from my mother's photo album, perhaps one of her departed uncles.

Dali may well be one of the few remaining practitioners of this half-century-old style of posing, yet I have to admit he's more regal than ridiculous. Dali is a clown, at least in public, but he conducts himself with stately decorum. He may be a screwball prince, but he is a *prince* all the same, as most everyone in Catalonia would agree.

For the camera crew he will stage events and provide extras, but he will not allow himself to be filmed in the style we usually call cinema verité. Unguarded or candid moments simply are not permitted to be recorded. His carefully crafted image, developed many years ago down to the waxed mustache, precludes showing the public any mundane aspect of his life. Dali must be seen as extraordinary all the time. His mercurial and taciturn wife, Gala, it is said, helped create this image for her husband as part of a public relations effort to make him famous.

The public Dali may be flamboyant and eccentric, or perhaps even a caricature of an eccentric, but the private Dali is well behaved, and he speaks good English, too. In public he affects the damnedest accent, sometimes perfectly incomprehensible, intermixed with what sounds like French idioms, or what may well be expressions of his own devising, as if he were inventing a new language. When we were alone with Dali, he spoke English perfectly.

Dali is, or was, a great painter. Many of his early paintings are brilliant, as can be viewed directly in the Teatro-Museo Dali in Figueras. I should quality that. There's one room in particular, a red plush-lined treasure vault in this year-old museum, filled with Dali-owned originals such as *Galarina, El Espectro de la Libido,* and *Cesta de Pan.* The rest of the museum is actually in continual flux, displaying unfinished works and art of uneven quality. We spent two days filming in the museum, which is about a 40-minute drive from Dali's home in Port Lligat. Port Lligat is actually the northeastern end of the town of Cadequez, where we spent two weeks filming Dali's activities and his environment.

We passed our first and last weeks in Spain in Barcelona at the Ritz, that terminal resting place of the rich come in out of the smog. Dali maintains a suite in the Ritz and holds nightly soirées which are emceed by one Verité, who allegedly runs a model agency. Verité provides the "extras" for the soirées, which take place in the early evening, right before dinner (dinner never comes too early in Spain).

Usually there are only two or three people at the soirées whom Dali considers to be of any importance. The rest of the cast is there for effect. Filmmakers make perfect extras, and Verité provides models, flamenco dancers, and many persons of demonstrable weirdness—so long as he, she, or it is passably chic.

And who is that gorgeous high-cheekboned, full-breasted French blonde? Why, that's Amanda. Ten years ago she was a top Paris model, and before that, they tell us, Amanda was a man. Now that you mention it, although I would never have suspected . . . or is this just a Dali put-on, some ploy designed to make us question the sexual origins of everyone present?

"Senor Dali, we'd like to introduce our soundman, Lenny Lipton." It's my first Dali handshake. Dali briefly touches the tips of his fingers to mine while looking to his left, I guess at the next person waiting in line to shake hands.

From time to time I have wondered at the reason for my existence, and this handshake opened the question for discussion once more. I shouldn't take any of this personally. Why take life personally if you can help it? Collectively, Dali calls us Le Crew. He calls the director of the film, landscape architect Lawrence Halprin, Le Architect, which is understandable enough. He calls Sue Yung Li Ikeda Le Chinese (not even La Chinese), and he dubs cinematographer Paul Ryan Polaroid.

Le Architect is designing the Dali museum to be built in Cleveland, which will hold some 90 original oils and other Dali works valued at some $25 million. The collection is owned by plastics-machine manufacturer Reynolds Morse, and Morse and his wife, Eleanor, were present during filming.

It was Morse who relayed to *Le Crew* ideas and instructions from Dali. Dali had many suggestions about what we should shoot, and he was actually quite pleased to have a film crew willing to spend time exploring his environment and the landscape that helped to shape his painterly sensibility. This is one of the goals of the film, which will become a resource of the Cleveland museum, where I assume it will be shown on a daily basis.

So it was that we spent a good part of our time trekking to places that Dali said were important to him—places where he and his family visited when he was a youth: the Roman ruins of Ampurius, a pond adjacent to a church outside of Figueras where Dali went potty as a three-year-old, the great tourist attraction of the monastery of Montserrat.

It was at Montserrat that Reynolds and Eleanor Morse were lost somewhere at the top of the mountain. At the fall of night, just as the monks were ready to begin their search, the Morses appeared singing and laughing. Although we had waited for them for hours, they did not consider themselves to be lost, since they knew where they were all the time.

I can see Reynolds and Eleanor skipping across the mountains of Spain like a pair of spry mountain goats, while we followed, burdened with 500 pounds of gear. First-rate guides, the Morses, but they don't like to stop to let you take pictures.

Since I've titled this article "Filming *Le Pink Grapefruit*," a few words about the production itself seem in order. I will concentrate on sound, since that's what I did.

Most of my experience as a filmmaker has involved doing all the production and postproduction work myself. So concentrating on a specialty like recording sound was a new challenge. My insights may be too green to help most experienced sound persons, but beginners may possibly find what I have to say to be of some value.

Cinematographer Ryan used an Eclair NPR for almost all the photography, with an occasional assist from a Bolex and a Beaulieu, often fitted with an Angenieux 5.9mm wide-angle lens. The Eclair was used, for the most part, with an Angenieux 9.5 to 95mm zoom lens. The entire film was shot on Eastman 7247 color negative stock. Tests conducted by Ryan before production started kept him from pushing more than a few hundred feet of the film.

Most of the production was shot with available light, but extensive setups were required within the Teatro-Museo Dali, using Lowel lights with transformers to turn the European 220-volt current into a usable 120 volts for our American units.

Like everybody else making movies, I have great respect for the Nagra recorders, but I didn't relish lugging a hefty 16 pounds across Spain. After two days of test shooting before we left for Europe, the pain in my shoulder told me the Nagra was too much of a burden. So I investigated the possibility of using a Stellavox SP7, and the people I asked about this alternative Swiss machine said terrible things about it. Now, it's curious that this attitude should be so widespread, since nobody I asked—people with strong opinions, I might add—had ever used a Stellavox, which looks a lot like a Nagra but is half its thickness and weight.

The SP7 I selected had a crystal reference for the pilot channel built in, and monaural heads, although there are two mike channels which can be mixed without an accessory mixer. Stellavox recorders are available in head configurations of two channels and three channels, and there are other options as well. The SP7 will also directly supply power for mikes like the Sennheiser 815 shotgun, which requires 9 volts DC. One feature of the SP7 is a low-frequency roll-off control, which is useful, for example, for suppressing traffic noise and which should always be used with the 815, since it has a tendency to emphasize unwanted lows and to produce whooshing sounds itself when in motion. I used the Sennheiser and Stellavox for 95 percent of the sound recording, and it was a pleasing combination, to say the least. The Stellavox worked great!

Despite the fact that the Sennheiser can make good recordings of comparatively distant subjects and pick out wanted sound from background noise, like every other mike, it must be used in as close to the subject as possible to get the best recordings. So I was left with the usual contradictory requirement of miking in close but keeping myself and the mike out of the shot. My years of experience working a camera helped me guess what focal lengths Ryan was using with the zoom lens. I had more trouble staying out of the shot when he was using the 5.9mm Angenieux, because of its wide coverage, but things worked out pretty well with a practically subliminal system of gestures and signals.

There is something about recording sound that lends itself to coolness and detachment. Hearing seems to take place deep inside the head, something fostered by those damned earphones you have to wear to ensure success. They may let you hear what the tape hears, but they create a barrier between the sound person and the world.

The sound person is also in a somewhat more precarious position with the director than the camera person because the sound person is usually the first bearer of bad news. For example, the sound person, unlike the cinematographer, can immediately hear any technical failure in recording. Often the film itself cannot be viewed for days (and in our particular case, for weeks), so if anything has gone wrong in filming, it is discovered in the cutting or screening room when it is too late.

Recording in the field is hazardous, to say the least, if top-quality sound is the goal. Witness all the postsync dubbing that is used in feature films shot on location, despite the fact that these crews usually use two or three people specializing in sound and equipment far more elaborate than anything we had. Nevertheless, it was a dreadful moment for me when I had to tell the director that we were getting lousy sound, either because of weirdly functioning equipment or because of terribly loud background sounds made by one of the world's numerous machines.

Sound stands in a stepchild relationship to image. The sound person doesn't often get praised for recording brilliant sound. It just rarely happens that anybody recognizes the importance of excellent sound until they hear really loused-up recordings. Superlatives are saved for great photography.

It's probably best to let the subject of our film have the final words here. I recall our last conversation with Dali in his outrageous garden at his home in Port Lligat. The garden looks like a set that has been dressed to make it appear to be part of a hippie pad, featuring plastic plants intermixed with live plants, a telephone booth near the barbecue pit, a Michy Michelin white plastic statue, and, in general, kitschy junk scattered here and there.

There he was—Dali, seated at the far end of the pool under a little canopied shelter on a great big stuffed pillow, telling us his message. Not satisfied with having communicated this wisdom once, he repeated it several times in perfect English, clear enough for anyone to understand: "After all of your suffering, you should throw the film in the garbage."

The Lowdown
on Super 8 Education

In the past few years, I've frequently consulted with people who are organizing filmmaking programs, and I've taught at a number of institutions. Although I think of myself as a filmmaker willing to work with any format that suits any particular project, I am considered an expert in the field of super 8 technology, undoubtedly because of my writing in *Super-8 Filmaker* and *The Super 8 Book*. Much of what I advise, then, has been drawn from the planning of super 8 filmmaking systems geared to the needs of institutions engaged in teaching the craft of this popular film format.

What follows is a generalization based on my particular experience. It may well be that I am encapsulating the institutional thinking vis-à-vis super 8, or perhaps I may not have a sufficiently broad or typical sample from which to extrapolate. In either case, my experience shows that there are two prevailing points of view in the blooming field of super 8 filmmaking education. The first sees super 8 as a stepping-stone or training ground for advancement to the larger "professional" formats; the second sees super 8 as a simplified medium that can be used by everyone.

In line with the first approach, all the techniques employed in 16 and 35mm are used in the production of super 8 films. This includes recording double-system sound with crystal-controlled or referenced cameras and recorders, transferring and mixing procedures well established in advanced practice, and editing techniques using multiple-reel motorized editing benches or sophisti-

120

cated horizontal editing decks. In addition, students are taught to use workprint and to conform their camera original to the workprint using the A-and-B roll scheme, which allows for invisible splices and dissolves.

I can't see why anyone who is taught super 8 filmmaking using the above approach could not, with a minimum of effort, work in larger formats. As a training medium, super 8 has the great advantage of relatively low-cost hardware (cameras and projectors), and its software (film and tape) costs far less than that of the larger formats. This last factor may prove more important in the long run to medium- to large-size teaching facilities, as well as to the students themselves.

The second major camp emerging in the world of super 8 filmmaking instruction favors a more democratic approach. While the first attitude is essentially aimed at turning out filmmaking specialists, or in a real sense, technological elitists, the second approach is designed to bring filmmaking to the people—to anybody and everybody. It is here that super 8 makes its unique contribution to twentieth-century communications, for it is a low-cost, easy-to-use, intimate medium allowing just about any individual to make a super 8 movie from the moment he or she is old enough to change a cartridge.

Essentially, this easy-does-it approach engages people who are not going to make filmmaking a livelihood, but who are going to use it to record their trip to Scotland, the work of their YMCA, women's group, community action projects, or whatever. Super 8 has the power to place the filmmaking medium in the hands of people—ordinary and extraordinary—who need to tell their story on film.

In classes and workshops on this kind of filmmaking, the emphasis is on single-system (sound-on-film) cameras and on cutting single system with simple editing machines. Often a sound striper will be used to apply stripe to film shot silent, so that sound can be dubbed directly with the aid of a magnetic sound projector. The added track most usually will be sound-over, narration, or music and sound effects.

Although I have been working with sophisticated 16mm equipment for years, and my own super 8 setup is nothing to sneeze at, my heart belongs to the filmmaking-for-everybody camp. It's one of the things I like most about the possibilities of super 8. It appeals to me, maybe because it's as American as a fast-food hamburger.

I would have no quarrel with the super 8-as-a-stepping-stone people if these folks didn't feel that this was the sole value of super 8 and so miss its potential. There is a fantastic degree of prejudice on the part of professional filmmakers and film instructors, maybe because they cut their teeth on 16 or 35mm. In their heart of hearts, they have scant respect for this preposterously tiny format. I have even encountered situations where instructors who have never made a super 8 film are telling students how to do it.

Super 8 actually requires more skill to turn out a decent film than the larger formats because the super 8 frame is so tiny. If the last drop of quality isn't present in the original photography and sound, and if all the postproduction operations aren't carried out meticulously, the finished film will suffer greatly. Super 8 filmmakers have to be consummate craftspeople.

I should add that there are three institutions that, as far as I know, in their programs regard super 8 to be a sophisticated means of film production in and of itself. These are the State University of New York in Buffalo, MIT, and Rice University.

There is no reason why people who are aspiring to make filmmaking their thing can't work with simple single-system cameras for many projects. It turns out that first-rate sound can be recorded with many of these instruments, and this streamlined approach can lead to heightened intimacy at the time of shooting. Double-system sound (sound and picture recorded with separate machines), while it can be done by one person, usually requires both camera person and sound recordist. I have found that there is a natural tendency for subjects to relate to the sound person instead of the camera person. This inevitably leads to a less direct, less intimate type of cinema. Single-system shooting, with a microphone mounted on the camera or as an integral part of the camera, elicits a more direct, one-to-one cinema, encouraging the subjects to express directly to the audience through the camera person. In addition, footage which has been shot single system may be carried through all the postproduction double-system procedures that are necessary to satisfy complicated cutting and sound techniques.

People who are approaching filmmaking as a means of personal communication but not necessarily as a way of life would similarly profit from an exposure to double-system cutting, for it is actually simpler than single-system cutting. It takes less effort, and you don't necessarily have to be extremely ingenious to do it. While dubbing directly to stripe with a magnetic projector can produce fine effects, all that cueing and direct mixing with sound-on-sound takes far more skill than simply cutting a separate magnetic film to correspond with the picture.

Yet, when all is said and done, the most powerful contribution of super 8 is the intimacy it adds to filmic expression. No other medium has its ability to peel away layers and show real people in daily situations. People who approach super 8 as a teaching tool only are exploiting super 8's economy and the fact that all the traditional filmmaking techniques can be used in this medium. But that's less important than super 8's unique filmmaking contribution: It is unintimidating. It's a form of filmmaking that is economical, not merely in terms of dollars and cents, but more importantly, in simplicity and directness of expression.

Section 4
Afterimage

Introduction:

The Man in the Victor Mature Jacket

Perhaps my concern with projection has gotten to be such a habit with me that strangers can actually smell it. When *Clockwork Orange* was first playing at the Metro in San Francisco, I attended a screening comfortably outfitted in my Victor Mature jungle white tux jacket with padded shoulders, giant lapels, two-button front, and pleated back with a vestigial belt sewn across the rear waist. Once, in a burst of foolish enthusiasm, after completing his famous Marlon Brando impersonation, Francis Coppola autographed the lining of this jacket.

The projection that evening at the Metro wasn't terribly good, what with framelines drifting here and there, but it came as a surprise to me, as I was leaving the theater with friends, to be stopped by a man who was obviously the manager. "Please," he said in a fawning and miserable tone, "please forgive the projection. There was a new man on tonight. The union . . . they give us whoever they like. Our regular projectionist is sick. Please, please. . . ."

His hand tugged at the sleeve of my wonderful white jacket. I couldn't resist speaking softly. "I won't tell Stanley. I'll forget it even happened."

The man thanked me. He was right to apologize for the miserable projection, and it was appropriate for me to relieve his anxiety. Compassion is a quality that comes naturally after great suffering in the motion picture theaters and private screening rooms of our land.

Toward the
Perfect Projector

Motion picture equipment manufacturers are a conservative lot. This is especially true of organizations that supply the higher-priced 16 and 35mm gear for professional or commercial filmmakers. It's a curious fact that an advance like reflex viewing (through-the-camera lens), which has always been a run-of-the-mill feature on super 8 cameras, has only in the last decade become standard on 35mm studio cameras. And features like automatic exposure control or the electronically controlled pull-down claw that is used on all super 8 sound-on-film cameras are still hard to find on large-format equipment.

You may have noticed that the examples I've mentioned pertain to cameras and not projectors, which may seem peculiar in an article devoted to the perfection of the projector. But the ironical point is that while super 8 cameras are, on balance, praiseworthy instruments and in some ways ahead of their bigger brothers, the super 8 projectors leave a great deal to be desired.

Super 8 projectors are usually used for projecting camera-original footage. This is the film that actually ran through the camera as opposed to a print made from that original, the practice for the larger formats. This means that extra-special care ought to go into designing the super 8 projector to reduce film wear. This just isn't the case, as far as I can tell, for the vast majority of super 8 machines.

But the projectors don't carry all the blame. Many conventional models, like the Eumig machines, will not scratch film if they are cleaned frequently. This means that access to the gate area in order to remove built-up emulsion that cakes on the aperture or pressure pad parts should be a factor in your buying decision. Needless wear and tear also takes place on editing viewers that are poorly designed in the first place, are out of alignment, or are improperly cleaned. And a great deal of harm stems from poor handling when winding film from reel to reel during editing. Make sure you don't cinch film, that is, tug one end to tighten it on the reel. By all means wind your film slowly and carefully. It's a good precaution to clean your film with a liquid cleaner and lubricant like Kodak Film Cleaner, Durafilm's Super Cine Clean, or ECCO's 1500.

It's depressing to relate, but the machines kindest to film, the Kodak Ektasound models 235 and 245, were discontinued early in 1977. They used a sprocketless system very similar to the drive systems used in super 8 sound-on-film cameras. The 235 and 245 were so easy on film, that you could actually thread them up with the film perforations on the wrong side—that is, opposite the pull-down claw —and the projectors wouldn't do any harm to the film. Make that mistake in the usual projector and you'll get a new row of perfs running through your sound track!

Although the toothed sprocket wheel can cause its share of damage to film, often the harm that befalls film takes place at the gate, where the pull-down claw engages the film at 18 or 24 frames each second. Here is a wonderful opportunity for producing scratched film, with emulsion and base rubbing against metal aperture parts. But more than this, the action of the claw will tend to wear the leading edge of the perforation, so that over a period of time the projected image becomes increasingly less steady. As wear continues, it becomes impossible to project the film.

At the October 1976 Society of Motion Picture and Television Engineers (SMPTE) convention in New York, I saw what could be the answer to the film-wear dilemma. There I had the opportunity to examine the Hollogon projection system, which does away with the claw, and the shutter to boot.

The heart of the Hollogon system is a device called a *skanner*, or *image immobilizer*. The skanner takes the place of both the claw and the shutter and serves analogous functions. Film runs continuously through the projector rather than being pulled or pushed one frame at a time into position behind the projector lens. The skanner dissolves frames, or blends them together, thereby eliminating the need for the shutter, whose function is to prevent the actual movement of film from being projected. The skanner, by its clever arrangement of 24 facing mirrors, captures, or "immobilizes," each projected frame, even though the frame is in motion. Each successive frame is blended together with a dissolve.

In the 35mm model demonstrated at SMPTE, the skanner was 5½ inches in diameter and was assembled from individual mirror segments cemented in place. In production, such an assembly might be replaced by aluminum mirrors. For smaller formats, plastic injection-molded skanners could be employed to remain cost competitive with the present film-advance mechanisms. For super 8, the device could be scaled down so that its diameter would be only 1 inch. The Hollogon Optical Systems Corporation (225 Park Avenue South, New York, New York 10003) plans to manufacture super 8 skanner units.

Using mirror optics or a reflecting prism for image stabilization is nothing new. For years, editing machines with viewers have employed prisms, which have resulted in a flickering image that is acceptable for these applications. The use of this kind of device to produce a projected image predates what we usually consider to be the invention of the motion picture camera itself. In 1877 and 1888, French inventor Emile Reynaud patented his Praxinoscope, in which a mirror drum was used to optically stabilize images that were on a hand-drawn material closely resembling today's film. Reynaud's Theatre Optique gave performances in Paris from 1892 until 1900, with Reynaud himself hand cranking the apparatus for every show. Conceptually, Reynaud's mirror drum is similar to today's image stabilizers or the Hollogon skanner.

The Hollogon projection system might well replace the pull-down claw and shutter in some super 8 projectors in the next few years. Not only will this virtually eliminate film wear, it will also make what is today called "instant slow motion" commonplace on sound projectors. Today, a super 8 filmmaker seeking slow motion *and* sound projection must buy two projectors. The Hollogon system also allows for still-frame projection and continuously variable rates up

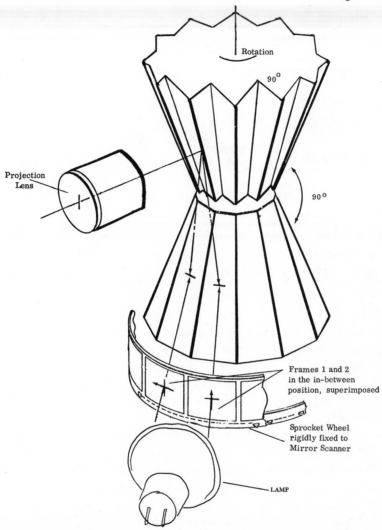

The Hollogon skanner—a single unit composed of front surface plane mirrors and sprocket wheel rigidly mounted to mirror scanner. Light passes through frames, is reflected by lower mirrors on roof scanner half (top), and then through projection lens.

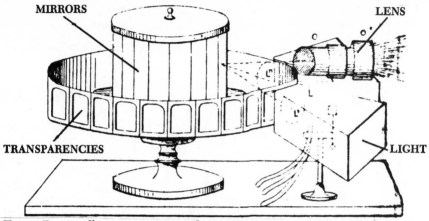

MIRRORS — LENS — TRANSPARENCIES — LIGHT

From Reynaud's patent, November 13, 1877, no. 4244. Hand-drawn transparencies are wrapped around a drum; light passes through them to a mirror surface, and then through projection lens onto screen.

to several hundred frames per second. This could greatly aid the film-maker in the editorial process.

As an added bonus, the continuous drive ought to result in a drastic reduction of projector mechanical noise. The annoying hum and clatter of present machines might well be reduced to tape recorder level.

In a conversation with the inventor of the Hollogon skanner, Ulrich Fritzler, I learned that the system has an optical limitation: its maximum speed in the super 8 form is $f/2.8$. If we use a lens faster than $f/2.8$, there will be no additional light on the screen. But this system will actually give the equivalent performance of a twice-as-fast $f/2$ optic, since there is no light loss owing to the blocking action of the shutter. In other words, the continuous blending action of the Hollogon, without shutter, produces a two-times increase in light output compared with an intermittent system employing a multi-bladed shutter. But the mirrors used in the skanner itself lower the effective f stop to $f/2.8$. Too bad.

The skanner may also be employed in videoplayer units. Unlike the present projection system, which employs a pull-down and a blackout for each projected frame, the dissolving action of the immobilizer is perfectly compatible with the scanning action of TV pickup devices. This could lead to a great simplification in design for the next generation of videoplayers, producing a reduction in size, weight, and, blessedly, cost.

At any rate, the future looks exciting, and I for one can hardly wait to start using the next generation of projection equipment. It's one thing to write about an advance like this, and quite another to play with it.

Comparing Super 8 and 16mm

Let's return to that recurring question, Exactly what are the differences between projected super 8 and 16mm? To put it succinctly, the 16mm image is sharper and brighter and has less grain and more saturated color than the super 8 image, whose better sound has less background noise and distortion with a fuller, richer frequency response.

I hope you realize a statement like that invites all kinds of qualifications. To begin with, I am not speaking about the results of laboratory experiments using special test apparatus and one-of-a-kind emulsions; nor am I talking about ancient machines projecting movie prints made decades ago. I'm comparing the range of super 8 and 16mm films as they are produced these days and projected with commonly available, modern assembly-line equipment.

I should emphasize that I am comparing system quality in terms of overall final results, that is, how super 8 and 16mm movies look and sound. I am not comparing costs, equipment design, or the typical working methods of the mediums.

For usual projection situations, super 8 still comes off second to 16mm in terms of the traditional criteria of image quality. That's because 16mm has a shade more than three times the image area, and all things being equal, image quality is proportional to area.

When I say *all things being equal*, I am assuming that if we are using a 16mm print (or original), we are also using a super 8 print (or original). But 16mm is more often a print medium, where a copy of the original film is shown, while super 8 encourages projection of

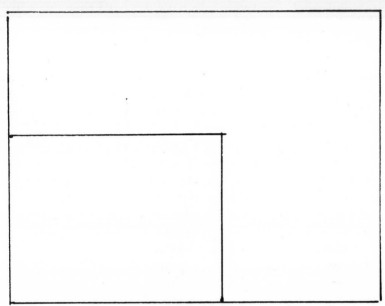

Comparison of super 8 and 16mm image area. The smaller super 8 frame is set into the larger 16mm frame.

camera original, that is, the actual film shot in the camera. In the past five decades, a printmaking system of camera film and print stock has been established to serve 16mm filmmakers. But there is no similar backup for super 8. If prints are your goal, the best you can do for most subjects in super 8 is to shoot on your favorite camera stock and print on Gevachrome 9.03.

Since 16mm is a printmaking medium while original super 8 film is commonly projected, a useful comparison would be one that shows a 16mm print with a super 8 original. This involves setting up two same-size screens side by side and projecting super 8 camera film next to a print of 16mm camera film.

Using standard modern projectors, the 16mm image—since it has three times super 8's area—is going to be three times brighter. Brighter projected images look sharper, so the 16mm film will look a lot better. However, most of this extra "quality" is due simply to the brighter image.

Okay, but what about video display, or what I sometimes like to call "electronic projection"? How do our comparisons stack up? We're going to use an Eastman super 8 videoplayer (model VP-1) to show our movies on a TV screen alongside a standard 16mm film chain, the kind used in most TV stations. While the VP-1's advanced method essentially converts movie images electronically into TV images, the film chain is a television camera that faces into a projector and picks up the image.

Despite the fact that the VP-1 costs about $1,700 and the film chain at least $15,000, the comparison is valid. With this equipment, it can be difficult to tell the difference between a super 8 camera original and a 16mm print. Even super 8 original and 16mm original can be difficult to tell apart. Equally interesting is that super 8 reduction prints from 16mm original compare very well with 16mm prints from the same original on the TV screen.

If we extend our conception of printmaking to include duplication of film to tape, we find that super 8 becomes a provocative production medium. In this country, 16mm is almost always transferred from prints, not original camera film. Super 8 *original* transferred directly to broadcast standard 2-inch tape or to other tape formats loses less quality than the usual 16mm route to tape. Therefore, super 8 can turn out to be a strong competitor as a production format for either tape distribution for closed-circuit viewing or for broadcast TV.

At the outset I asserted that super 8 magnetic sound (using a technology similar to the audio cassette) is better than 16mm optical sound (which is a photographic record of sound). This can be true even if we compare modern projectors playing back the best-quality tracks. But, commonly, super 8 is likely to be screened on recent equipment, while 16mm equipment was in all likelihood made in the last few decades. Under these circumstances, super 8 will sound even better. It seems hard to believe that a well-prepared super 8 magnetic track is superior to a similarly prepared 16mm optical track, but my repeated listening experience bears this out. Let's follow the production chain for both tracks and see if we can find the answer.

Both are usually magnetically recorded: 16mm usually employs

¼-inch reel-to-reel tape traveling at 7½ inches per second (ips), while super 8 sound is probably single-system Ektasound cartridges or cassette tape at 1⅞ ips or mag film at either 3 or 4 ips (18 or 24 fps). Then there's a series of duplication steps in which reel-to-reel tape is transferred to mag film, or cassette to mag film, or Ektasound cartridge to mag film; then a further dubbing in which mag tracks are mixed and equalized (manipulation of the audio spectrum to improve, or sweeten, the sound). Finally, the super 8 film is dubbed from the mag film master to striped print film, and the 16mm mag film is converted to 16mm optical track for prints. Until this last printing stage, the 16mm track retains its quality. But after this stage, you'll find that, although print losses for super 8 mag film track are minimal, print losses for 16mm optical track are severe.

Optical sound can be as good as and maybe better in theory than magnetic sound. The trouble is that 16mm optical tracks have been locked into print standards set up by the theatrical film industry in the thirties, and they have not been upgraded until very recently.

Lately there has been a movement in the industry to improve the lot of 16mm sound. Witness the introduction of improved master optical track material from Agfa-Gevaert, stereophonic sound from Kodak, and noise reduction by Dolby. However, today's super 8 magnetic track can have less distortion, fuller frequency response, and less background noise than 16 or 35mm optical tracks. So, with quality equipment and stripe, you may be able to produce super 8 sound tracks superior to what you hear from feature films in your neighborhood theater.

The Bright Light

Looking for a very bright super 8 projector for that 10- to 20-foot screen? For the first screening of my film *Revelation of the Foundation*, at the Pacific Film Archive of the University of California at Berkeley, I borrowed the prototype Marc-300 Elmo ST 1200 conversion from Valley Projection and Camera (2227 West Olive Avenue, Burbank, California 91506). This consists of a Marc-300 metal arc projection lamp fitted directly into the Elmo projector. Here's how it works: In a conventional lamp, a filament glows and gives off light. In the metal arc lamp, there are two metal filaments (an anode and a cathode) with a spark between them. The illumination comes from glowing ionized gas in between the filaments.

Valley claims that the 300-watt metal arc lamp (which costs $50) that replaces the 21-volt/150-watt lamp (which costs $20) is 475 percent brighter! There's no question that the improvement is substantial. The matte surface screen at the Pacific Film Archive is about 15 feet wide, and like many other screens used in motion picture theaters, it's perforated to allow free passage of sound through it from loudspeakers. The perfs and the matte surface probably absorb, or lose, some 25 percent (or more) of the light falling on the screen. Nonetheless, the image projected by the Marc-300 was very bright.

It's doubtful whether a super 8 projector needs to be brighter than this unit. After all, how big do you want to blow up this minute frame? On the Archive screen, the super 8 image was magnified almost 1,000 times—the equivalent of a 35mm theatrical film shown on a 65-foot-wide screen.

Very little factory adaptation had to be done to the ST 1200, since cooling is just about adequate as is. The photo of the ST 1200 in the "Sound Projector Guide" section looks like the conversion except that the power supply, about the size of a typewriter, is not shown. The cooling path was changed slightly, and a new bracket for the lamp was installed. Most of the unit's $1,500 cost is for the power supply, which produces voltage high enough to ignite the arc, and then ballast circuitry to provide power smooth enough to prevent sending the lamp to an early grave. The projector runs hotter to the touch with the Marc-300, and I wouldn't advise using the single-frame feature of the Elmo unless you like roasted frame.

With the 1,200-foot capacity of the Elmo, and the optional $f/1.4$, 25 to 50mm zoom lens for projecting from the rear of many of the larger auditoriums, I'd say that this conversion could make large-screen projection a routine happening for super 8. Elmo has shown their own factory-produced metal arc projector in Japan, based on the ST 1200, the Grand, but they have no plans to offer it in this country. F & B/Ceco (315 West 43d Street, New York, New York 10036 and 7501 Santa Monica Boulevard, Hollywood, California 90038) has a similar Elmo conversion, which I hear works well (I haven't used it).

The Videoplayer

I recently had an opportunity to use an Eastman videoplayer, the VP-1, for six weeks in my living room. During that period, my family and I completely gave up optical projection. At first, the relative novelty of the machine, which can display the super 8 image on any TV set, had a lot to do with our enjoyment of it. But the enjoyment of viewing movies of friends and family in color—with sync sound—on our own TV set didn't seem to diminish.

Some months before I had use of the VP-1 in my home, I had used a VP-1 at the regional Kodak center on Van Ness Avenue in San Francisco. The unit I had at home seemed to be a moderate improvement over the first one I had used. Some of the difference may be attributed to my TV, which I think has a better image than the Kodak-owned machine on Van Ness. But judging from the appearance of the bread boards inside the machine on which the electronics are mounted, a great deal of the improvement probably lies in changes that were made to the VP-1 circuitry—changes which involved considerable modification to the electronics after the initial pass down the assembly line.

While the first VP-1 I used tended to flutter and roll a bit at splices, the new unit remained relatively steady, even when it encountered tape splices with wide gaps. The steadiness of the machine, using the SMPTE steadiness test, was fair to good at 18 fps and good to very good at 24 fps. This, too, was an improvement over the earlier VP-1.

A properly adjusted TV displaying the VP-1 image left little to be desired in comparison with programs broadcast over the air. I would judge sharpness to be adequate and color to be good. I came to this conclusion after making direct comparisons of various types of super 8 films with new programs, taped TV, locally originated feature films, and network-originated series and movies. My judgment corresponds with the consensus of opinion of the many people who viewed the VP-1 at work in my home.

I would say that Ektachrome 40 produced the best overall image. Although the E40 image is slightly grainier than Kodachrome, it gave a better range of gradation. Some people preferred the Kodachrome look, but the E40 when used in conjunction with the similar E160 makes for a formidable combination of two intercutable low- and high-speed emulsions. Too bad Eastman has discontinued E40 in this country. It ain't fair!

I also like the image I got with SM Ektachrome 7244, a low-contrast, moderately grained material which can capture delicate colors. It would make the perfect newsfilm for TV stations shooting super 8. Whatever super 8's advantages may be in terms of TV news gathering, it's being passed over (foolishly, I might add) for ENG (electronic news gathering) equipment, which consists of portable color TV cameras and recorders.

The VP-1 would be the perfect instrument for bringing home movies to the TV screen, and I believe that when we get a more portable and less expensive machine, viewing super 8 on the TV set will be the preferred projection method. (The present unit weighs 45 pounds and costs $1,700—too much weight and too many dollars for this application.)

Who knows what feat of technology will be required to produce a 20-pound $400-list videoplayer? When it can be done, it's curtains for optical projection for just about every home moviemaker.

But the applications of the VP-1 go far beyond home movies. SM Ektachrome, which may be processed very rapidly in the SM processor ($13,000), would, as I have said, make a splendid TV newsfilm. Another model of the videoplayer, the VP-X, is similar to the VP-1 but has an output that can be locked in sync to the signal of a TV station for broadcasting.

The VP-X could also be used for transferring super 8 to any tape format. Such transfers should be done with original camera film,

Eastman VP-X looks just like the VP-1, but is designed for use by TV stations or for direct duplication from super 8 film to tape, using a videotape recorder.

since the filmmaker could then color correct the footage. In many cases, I was able to take footage that had improper filtration and restore the color balance to produce a pleasing image.

When used in the single-frame mode, the VP-1 produced still images that were of outstanding quality. Moreover, two videoplayers locked in sync could be used for A and B rolling super 8 (in which two pieces of film are used) to produce dissolves or superimpositions, as I saw done by Stan VanDerBeek at the University of Maryland. VanDerBeek and his colleagues have the most advanced setup using VP-Xs that I know of, and the creative possibilities of using super 8 film for image manipulation are very exciting.

The Clean Sound

The payoff for every super 8 moviemaker is that moment when the room lights are dimmed and the projector is turned on. Guests and family are full of anticipation, their eyes riveted to the screen. No matter what you show them, for the first few minutes at least, you've got their attention. After that it's up to your skills as a filmmaker. Here I'm going to concentrate on one aspect of this entertainment problem—not what's on the screen, but what's coming out of your loudspeakers.

With a silent super 8 projector, you can run in tandem, although not in exact sync, any reel-to-reel or cassette tape recorder. The projector and tape recorder must be started together so that the image and sound will start more or less in sync. Exact synchronization is out of the question in a setup like this for a number of reasons. Tape is capstan driven and film is sprocket driven. Tape can slip between the metal cylinder, which is the capstan shaft, and the rubber snubber pushing against it. A tape nominally 10 minutes in length can run for 10 minutes and 5 seconds, or sometimes 9 minutes and 50 seconds, because of changes in temperature which affect the length of the tape. There are relatively elaborate means for electronically synchronizing a recorder and a projector, but for many applications, rough sync is just fine. (Music, for example, may not have to be precisely in sync.) However, for the utmost in convenience, reliability, and repeatability, the best way to add sound to your super 8 film is by using magnetically striped film and a sound projector.

The film can come prestriped, as it is in the sound-on-film Ekta-sound cartridges, or it can be poststriped after processing. In post-striping, the film is returned to the lab for the application of a magnetic sound stripe, some 27 thousandths of an inch wide, opposite the edge with the perforations. Many labs, Kodak especially, will also apply a balance stripe, some 12 thousandths of an inch wide, adjacent to the perforations. There are many projectors on the market that can use this balance stripe. It can be used for recording too, but its original purpose was to permit even winding of striped film on the take-up reel. Both stripes are about 0.4 thousandths of an inch above the surface of the film, which doesn't sound like much, but if you wind a few hundred feet of film on a reel, there will be a pileup on the striped edge and a corresponding sag on the unstriped edge. Working with striped film is almost exactly the same as working with magnetic sound tape. Your film becomes a dual medium for image and sound, and many super 8 sound projectors will allow you to record as well as play back.

As far as super 8 sound goes, the greatest stumbling block to what people usually call "high-fidelity" sound is mechanical noise. Super 8 cameras and projectors are noisier than tape recorders, but usually less noisy than 16mm equipment. When recording sound with a sound-on-film camera or playing it back on any super 8 sound projector, it's the mechanical noise that limits the fidelity of the sound more than anything electronic. My experience with super 8 sound projectors (which are invariably in the same room with the screen)

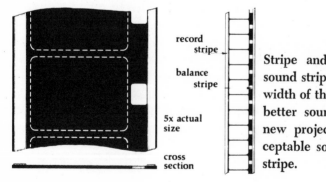

record stripe

balance stripe

5x actual size

cross section

Stripe and balance stripe. The sound stripe, more than twice the width of the balance stripe, yields better sound quality, but better new projectors can produce acceptable sound from the balance stripe.

has taught me that these projectors generally have about the same level of mechanical noise.

Why not take the projector out of the room? This is inconvenient in most home setups, although some people have gone to the trouble of cutting a hole in a closet door and projecting from within the closet through a glass port. Eliminating projector noise by some such means frees us to examine other factors influencing the sound system.

Most of us who make movies also own hi-fi or stereo sound equipment and are familiar with high-fidelity sound. We know that sound originating from a tape or record is clean and without distortion and has a full frequency response, from low notes to very high notes. In addition, hi-fi sound is free from wow and flutter—audible sound irregularities that can, in severe cases, sound like gargling.

How does super 8 sound compare? Well, first of all, hi-fi sound systems will be able to record or reproduce sounds from about 40 to 15,000Hz (cycles per second), whereas run-of-the-mill cameras can do a good job only from about 200 to 5,000Hz. The important point here, however, is that the human voice falls well within these limits. Sound cameras are fine for recording people talking.

If the camera runs very quietly or is sound blimped (put into a padded box), recording with clean sound will result. Another way to lower the background noise of the camera's motor and drive system is to place the microphone and subject as far as possible from the camera. But, for now, it is fair to say that in typical situations, the overall noise of super 8 lip-sync systems is well matched; that is, the typical projector noise will mask the camera noise.

Second, super 8 cameras or projectors that run well—or those which have been well tuned in a repair shop—should not produce audible wow or flutter. However, there is a great deal of difference between design and execution. No modern super 8 sound camera or projector *should* have wow or flutter. But in terms of execution— what happens on the assembly line—well, that's something else. It's important to realize that the standards for wow and flutter are much lower for the human voice than for music recording. In fact, I have used a number of machines which were perfectly fine for voice but troublesome for longer, sustained notes of music. If you hear any

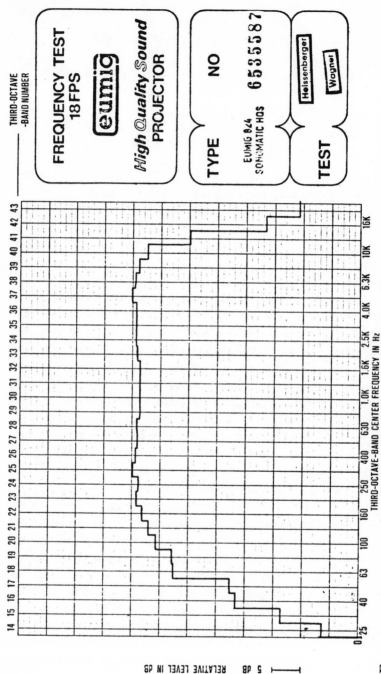

Frequency response test chart comes packed in the shipping container of the Eumig 824 Sonomatic HQS projector. This particular unit runs at 18 fps and has a response of 100 Hz to better than 10,000 Hz within plus or minus 2 dB. Somewhat higher frequency response should be expected at 24 fps.

speed irregularities in any part of your super 8 sound system, get it tuned by a good repair person or buy new equipment. (Weak batteries and dirty soundheads are also a source of wow and flutter for camera-recorded sound.)

Third, typical specifications for super 8 projector frequency response are set at about 80 to 8,000Hz (with an even narrower range for the camera) as opposed to the hi-fi standards of usually 40 to 15,000Hz. The super 8 sound doesn't abruptly fall off at its limits, however, since the reduction in frequency response is gradual. Moreover, the "missing" 40 cycles of low frequency and 7,000 cycles of high frequency do not have that much sound information anyway. Compared to high-fidelity standards, only the lowest and the highest octaves are lost. (An octave is a doubling in frequency response; so, from 40 to 80Hz is an octave, as is 8,000 to 16,000Hz.) As far as listening tests go, when playing back super 8 sound from a good projector, the frequency response is barely distinguishable from high-fidelity sound. I strongly recommend playing back your super 8 sound tracks through your hi-fi equipment. The trend in super 8 design allows us to consider the projector as a high-fidelity component.

Fourth, it is difficult to tell the difference between super 8 sound playback at 18 fps and playback at 24 fps. Practically speaking, a projector which has no wow or flutter at 24 fps will perform just as well at 18 fps. The same is true for frequency response. Although some qualification can be made here with regard to music, my assertion is perfectly true for voice recordings.

Finally, the most serious source of unwanted system sound, or noise, is hum. Some super 8 projectors have too high a background hum level to qualify as hi-fi sound. Their magnetic soundheads have to be very sensitive pickup devices to play back (and record) good-quality sound. This also makes them all too likely to pick up unwanted hum generated by the relatively powerful projector motors. Although the hum level may be low, and will rarely be heard in typical projection situations where the projector is in the same room as the audience and the screen, it's this hum that often is keeping the otherwise very good super 8 sound from being truly high-fidelity.

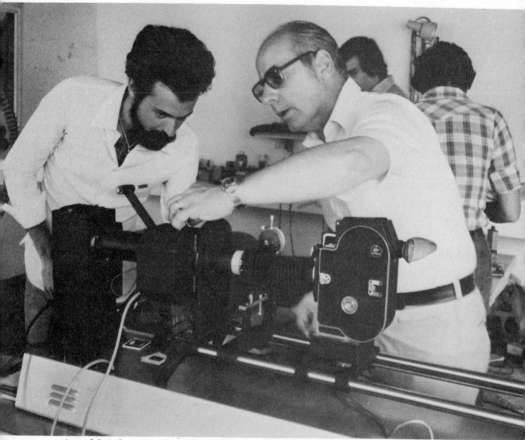

Arnold Scheiman (right) examines a J & K optical printer used by Venezuelan filmmaker Andy Valencia.

King of the Super 8 Blowup

Arnold Schieman is an open-minded optimist. He's also the senior technical consultant of the Canadian National Film Board. As Schieman describes it, he has overcome a number of professional prejudices, starting with "If you want a good motion picture image, better use 35mm." That's the way he felt too, until he blew up the 16mm feature *Nobody Waved Goodbye* to 35mm, more than a decade ago.

"I told them I'd eat my shirt if it came out okay. I expected grain the size of golf balls. But when I screened the first blowup footage, I got out the ketchup." Schiemen has been improving his blowup process ever since, and now he's blowing up super 8 to 35mm. The results have astonished even this optimist.

When TV came to Canada's Northwest Territories, it was "Leave It to Beaver" and "I Love Lucy"—hardly relevant programming for whale hunters. So several years ago, the Canadian Film Board became interested in having people like Eskimo hunter Mosha Michael of Frobisher Bay produce films for TV transmission. Once again, Arnold was called in to do the blowups, this time from super 8 to 16mm.

Despite the fact that he was able to produce adequate 16mm prints from super 8 originals, Schieman was dissatisfied with the quality he was getting. He could feel in his bones that there was more in that super 8 frame than conventional printing techniques were able to reproduce. Moreover, the films of Mosha Michael had

149

the most difficult footage to blow up to 16mm, since many of the shots were of extremely high contrast—Eskimos in dark furs against brilliantly sunny, snow backgrounds.

At first, the Film Board used Ektachrome 40 as its original film stock. But Schieman found he could not get consistent quality processing for this stock; the lab-processed footage had marked shifts in color from cartridge to cartridge. So the Film Board switched to Kodachrome 40, which, as processed by Kodak, gives remarkably consistent roll-to-roll quality.

Still Schieman was not satisfied with the results. The problem, in a word, was contrast. Contrast buildup is an intrinsic part of photographic reproduction. When super 8 was blown up to 16mm, highlights were washed out and shadow detail was lost. The procedure was to go from super 8 camera original to 16mm internegative stock, which was then used as a master for producing 16mm positive-print film.

Usually no contrast correction is possible when printing color film, so Schieman decided that as an alternative he would go to an electronic or video intermediary for contrast reduction. In other words, the super 8 camera film would be put through a video film chain (see "Comparing Super 8 and 16mm") and turned into a TV image, which may be turned directly into 16mm printing masters or stored on videotape.

Schieman obtained a machine made by Teledyne called the Trinascope, a joint-effort design on the part of Teledyne and Kodak. The Teledyne process uses a Kodak M 100 TV projector that projects original film into a color TV camera that transforms the film image into green, blue, and red electronic signals, which can be individually manipulated for better contrast. The improved image is displayed on a high-quality TV monitor with specially selected color phosphors, ensuring color purity and accuracy. Finally, the TV screen is filmed by a special 16mm camera.

Schieman is able to separate the individual layers of the triple-layered (tripack) color film we use in our super 8 cameras. He can electronically manipuate each layer for contrast and color. The result, even at this early stage, is a super 8 blowup with very good color and contrast. The next step is to improve the resolution by increasing the number of lines per TV field from the 525 now used to 1,000 or more, to gain additional sharpness. Schieman is now working with both Kodak and Teledyne in an effort to improve the hardware for even finer super 8 blowups, or even good super 8 to super 8 prints.

Arnold Schieman comes on strong about super 8's image quality. He states emphatically that good blowups to 35mm or even 70mm are possible using the right techniques, an opinion that presently is heresy in the world of motion picture technologists. But I've seen his super 8 to 35mm blowups, and the results are astonishingly good. Schieman sounds like a vocal radical speaking out on behalf of super 8. He decries the conservatism of many of his colleagues who think of super 8 as if it were unfit for serious projects—as if it's a second-rate medium. Many of us know better, but Schieman has the blowups to prove it.

According to him, when screening original film, most super 8 image quality is lost in the projection optics. Given improved super 8 projectors, he envisions a substantial advance in on-screen quality. As an expert in lab procedures, Schieman's opinions on that point of the state-of-the-art are particularly relevant. He simply thinks that labs are not doing their best with super 8 prints and that, in some cases, they are overcharging for their services. Lab services for blowups are also excessive, and present pricing practices are likely to "kill the goose that laid the golden egg."

Schieman's position at the Film Board has put him squarely in the corner of the super 8 independent filmmaker, and it's no small thing to have him on our side. While at the second Super 8 Avant Garde International Film Festival in Caracas, Venezuela, in 1977, I had the chance to talk with him at length. He is the most zealous and outspoken, even maniacal, super 8 chauvinist I've found yet. He has what I began to think of as a Jor-El complex. Superman's father, Jor-El, you may recall, was an eminent scientist on the planet of Krypton, who attempted to convince the people of his world that it was about to blow up. But they did not listen to Jor-El. Schieman's blowup is not apocalyptic, even if most of his professional colleagues still discount his message.

Bringing Damaged Film
Back to Life

Since most of us super 8 filmmakers work with original camera film, we're all concerned with keeping our films free of damage from things like abrasions, scratches, torn sprocket holes, sprocket tooth marks punched into the film, lamp burns, tears, creases, or broken film. White, yellow, or green lines running down the length of the film means that it may have curled excessively, shrunk, gotten oil stained, or become brittle. These and a few more ghastly items are part of the checklist that returns with your film if you've had it treated by Film Life, Inc. (141 Moonachie Road, Moonachie, New Jersey 07074).

Film Life is one of the two organizations offering restoration of damaged super 8 film. The other is Rapid Film Technique (37–02 27th Street, Long Island City, New York 11101). So it was with great interest that I sent Film Life 1,200 feet of a film I had been working on for some time, *Children of the Golden West*. This was the first film I shot and edited in super 8, and you might say that I cut my super 8 teeth on it.

Children of the Golden West went through many a projector and many an editing machine, and with it I explored many possible techniques for handling super 8 original. I worked with the original because I've always found it a bit difficult to do carefully planned tests. The way I learn best is to get involved in a project and take it from there. Of course, it's possible to get terrible results when using new techniques, but working this way, I am motivated to do my best. When it came time to have this particular film printed, however, I had a scratched, abraded, dirty master that made a scratched, abraded, dirty-looking print.

It's only fair to say that audiences don't seem bothered by these beauty marks, but the first time through the projector, my brand-new print looked like one that was worn out. People may not mind the appearance of such a film because they are used to seeing motion picture prints that are in sorry shape. Nevertheless, it pained me to see what had happened to my film.

So I arranged for Marvin Bernard, president of Film Life, to have a go at *Children*. He did, and the results are nothing short of superb. I can verify this simply by comparing the restored original with a print of the film made from the unrestored original, which serves as a complete record of scratches, abrasion, and so on. For the most part, the film is now free of blemishes. A few defects, such as occasional greenish tram lines have not been entirely eliminated. But these are the result of layers of emulsion which have been gouged away, and nothing can be done to replace this missing picture infortion. So you should bear in mind that some defects can be eliminated and others have to remain.

Film Life evaluates each film for particular defects and then gives it the appropriate treatment, which costs 10 cents per foot for black-and-white film and 15 cents per foot for color. I was warned that the process might damage magnetic sound track, but in the case of my film, I had already made a mag film dupe of the sound for making prints. Despite the fact that my returned master's sound track was undamaged, I would advise you to take suitable precautions.

Since Mr. Bernard knew that I would be writing about his process, there's always the danger that my film may have received extra-special handling. I don't believe this was the case.

Protecting
Your Film

Although my films get screened publicly, as well as in my living room, their subject matter makes them resemble home movies. My films dig into daily life and show how my friends and family are passing through this strange world. And I've learned as much from home-movie techniques as I have from commercial filmmakers.

Until a few years ago, I worked almost exclusively in 16mm, using the traditional approaches inherited from commercial practices. It's not that I hadn't questioned these techniques; it's simply that a large part of the time I wanted to do the same kinds of things the professionals were doing. For example, it is usually frowned upon to cut original 16mm camera film directly. One makes a workprint to take the beating in the course of day-to-day editing while the original rests safely in a can on a shelf until the editing process is complete. Then it is carefully matched to the workprint and is used for printing only.

So, when I fell in love with super 8, I asked myself if I could break away from a decade of 16mm experience and work like the home moviemaker. The answer to a question like this can always be yes if one is willing to alter the standard of quality one has gotten used to. Would the continual handling of super 8 film cause abrasions and scratches, not to mention downright damage and destruction? What would happen to those dangerously narrow super 8 perforations in the course of editing? How could I add to a shot I had cut too short without showing an obvious splice? I think that over the last few years I have satisfied myself on every point, and I have mastered an absolutely direct way to work with original camera film.

In the process of editing a film, I probably screen it at least a hundred times. So the first problem I had to deal with was how to prevent scratches? Where do scratches come from? If there is a burr, or raised edge, where film comes in contact with a stationary part of the projector or editing equipment, the film will get scratched. The best way to check out equipment for a burr is to run some black leader through it. Black leader has a maximum emulsion density, and any scratches will certainly be revealed. (You can make black leader yourself by covering your lens with a lens cap and shooting as much as you need.) Run the leader through the projector with the emulsion toward the lens. That's the way the camera original would be projected.

If you put a sufficiently long length of film through the projector and splice it end to end, you'll have a continuous loop which can be run for five or ten minutes. (You should be able to run such a loop through your projector for an hour without any marring or scratching.) Look for scratches on the base and emulsion sides of the film with a low-power magnifying glass.

Suppose you find that your projector *is* scratching your film. It is a relatively simple matter to introduce leader into the projector and isolate the scratch-producing part. Run a few inches in, and run it out. No scratch? Well, run a few more inches in and out, and then you can see just where the scratch begins. Usually it's in the gate. If you can remove the gate of your projector, you may be able to see the burr causing the damage.

It's curious that the same emulsion so easily scratched can be damaging to itself if it builds up on a portion of the gate. It can and will gouge out emulsion in a terrible cycle of emulsion buildup and film destruction. You can check for this by running the film past a clean white cloth dampened with film cleaner to see if any material comes off. If you are running a striped film, a moderate amount of brownish material from the stripe is all right. So is gray dust. Dust is a part of life and won't ruin your film. But watch out for the orange-colored stuff. That's emulsion dust, and it's killing your film.

Whether the problem is a burr or emulsion buildup, you will probably have to clean the gate. This can be done with denatured alcohol or shellac thinner. Moisten a cotton swab or flannel cloth with the alcohol and rub away. If the problem is a metal burr, back to the repair shop.

You can also try using 3 feet of Protect-A-Print leader at the head of your footage to clean the gate and help prevent emulsion buildup. It won't do much about dust, but dust, as I have said, doesn't cause scratches. Run the same kind of checks on your viewer, since this can damage film as badly as a projector.

One of the most important steps I took to protect my film was to give up cement splices. The dust and grit produced as they are being made can cause a lot of wear. The coarse emulsion and base particles can grind away at the film like sandpaper. Tape splicing for me has been the answer for one additional reason: film can be added to restore a cut shot without anyone noticing the splice. Cement splices use up a frame or two when you remake a splice; this can produce an unwanted jump in the image. Not so with tape. I suggest you investigate the Fuji ($17) tape splicer, which makes high-quality tape splices that cover both sides of the film without covering the mag stripe. Only one frame on either side of the frameline is covered, for a maximum visibility, two-frame splice.

After every editing session, or after several projections, wipe your film clean with an antistatic record cloth moistened with film cleaner; you may be impressed with the amount of stuff that comes off. Several brands of cleaner with lubricant are on the market, or you could use disposable wipes together with a cleaner. Don't use a dry cloth; moisten it to make it damp but not sopping. Apply light, steady pressure to the film as you move it through the folded cloth, cleaning base and emulsion sides at once. Wind the film slowly, with the cleaning cloth near the feed reel so that there's room for evaporation before the film is taken up on the rear reel. Wet film taken up produces a beaded or streaky effect that's hard to get off.

The chemicals in today's film cleaner are less toxic than they used to be, as the ghosts of lab rats will testify. But don't take chances. Open windows, use a fan, and don't clean a lot of film at one time. Keep film clean, but save your lungs.

I haven't mentioned to you my most controversial proposal for handling film: give up cotton editing gloves. You see, it is next to impossible to make tape splices and use cotton gloves. I clean my hands every so often with pop-up baby wipes. So help me, it works great. And the proof is in the projection.

I would also like to suggest that you get your film Peerless or Vacuumate treated. These processes toughen the film and lubricate it; they work very well. Most any professional motion picture lab will take care of this for you at a low cost. Striped footage can be given the total treatment, but unstriped film that you plan to have striped must *not* be lubricated, since this can prevent binding of the stripe. The lubricating step can be performed after striping, or you can stripe the film first and go all the way with either the Vacuumate or Peerless processes.

Eastman claims that the "rail effect," or the holding of emulsion away from the base by the raised balance and record stripe, can prolong the life of the film. Maybe so, but oxide particles can accumulate between the layers, and if you cinch your film—that is, yank on the film to tighten it—it's like sandpapering it. Never do anything like this. If your film has been sloppily wound on your reel, rewind it.

Working with originals would give professionals the willies. Thank God we are not professionals with their built-in prejudices. Editing super 8 camera film has cut my cost by about a sixth or seventh. It has forced me to make up my mind about each cut. There is a certain cleanness and clearness about working with original camera film with my naked hands that I never got with 16mm.

Making Prints

Super 8 may be many things to many people, but to most of us it isn't a medium for making prints. Yet, if you don't make prints, eventually your film can be seriously damaged or rendered unprojectable because of wear.

Eastman Kodak, for one, provides for the home moviemaker what is probably a perfectly adequate printmaking service for both silent and sound movies. Kodak duplicates the original film on an Ektachrome 7389 print stock.

I've had very good experiences with Kodak and their recent printmaking efforts. In particular, Ektasound or other magnetic sound camera original is printed at a cost of 28 cents per foot, including sound duplication onto mag-striped print stock. The major drawback of the Kodak services is the lack of *timing* (scene-to-scene exposure correction)—a routine service at any professional motion picture laboratory. Scene-to-scene or shot-to-shot exposure correction, which is accomplished by controlling the intensity of the printer's source of illumination, can mean the difference, especially if there are uneven exposures, between a lousy and a first-rate print.

Eastman is now printing customers' super 8 films on 7389, a low-contrast stock. I believe this will be replaced in the near future by the improved 7399 print stock, which at this moment, is made only in France and not available with super 8 perfs.

Compared with the original camera material, the 7389 print showed just the slightest increase in grain and a very slight decrease in sharpness. Skin tones tended either to go somewhat pale for subjects with light skin or ruddy for darker-skinned people. Shadow detail held up well, and highlights hardly washed out. Most colors stayed on target, with only slight shifts that most people wouldn't notice. Registration of the print was very good.

The original camera material was Ektachrome 160. I did not have an opportunity to do a test on Kodachrome film. Sound quality was somewhat off the mark from tests made three years ago at Kodak Park (all super 8 prints are done in Rochester). Output was lower than it needed to be, and there was a noticeable loss of high-frequency response. There was also dropout at the splice points of the original.

My overall impression is this: For well-exposed camera film, Kodak is making very good prints. If the new '99 stock lives up to expectations, they could be setting the standard for super 8 duplication (assuming the quality of their sound transfer improves).

Aside from the Kodak service, here's what I can tell you from personal experience: My suggestions are, naturally enough, suited to my needs, and not necessarily yours. I have completed eight super 8 films, which have a running time of more than four hours, and in the course of making these films, I have shot on practically every stock generally available to the super 8 filmmaker. I have had prints made by a number of laboratories on several kinds of print stock. There are less than half a dozen organizations in North America that consider themselves to be super 8 motion picture specialists, and from what I have seen, their prints are more alike than different in quality. I therefore feel qualified to comment on the super 8 scene with regard to printmaking in general, although much of my experience has been with a local lab, Leo Diner Films of San Francisco.

Let's get into the subject of print quality a little more. Print quality can be measured in two areas, image and sound. Let's discuss image quality first.

One point that's often overlooked is that the super 8 filmmaker, unlike the 16mm worker, becomes familiar with the look of the original camera film and not with a workprint made from it. Thus the super 8 filmmaker must compare the *print* of the completed film with a memory of the higher-quality *original* camera film (not a *workprint*). Of course, audiences looking at the super 8 print have never seen the original, so they won't know what they're missing. If you've made a good film, they'll be looking at the film. So the first *secret,* as I see it, of successful super 8 printmaking is to make a good film.

The 16mm worker has at his or her disposal camera materials which are part of a manufacturer-established printmaking system comprising both camera film and specially matched print stock. No such system exists for the super 8 filmmaker. But the saving grace has been the introduction, in the last few years by both Kodak and Agfa-Gevaert, of low-contrast print stocks designed to work nicely with higher-contrast projectable camera original. So there are two print stocks—Gevachrome 9.03 and, at present, Ektachrome 7389— which will work fairly well in conjunction with just about any super 8 camera original.

Both Gevachrome 9.03 and the as yet unobtainable in super 8 perf 7399 were introduced in 1977. I have had a lab optically print super 8 camera film on 16mm 7399 print stock, making sure to fill an area the super 8 frame size. Next I projected this with a 16mm projector. Given the limitations of the test procedure I used (because of the unavailability of super 8 perforated Eastman 7399), I think it will prove the finest print stock Eastman has offered. In terms of grain and D-max (maximum black density), it produced richer, better-looking prints than the 7389.

As for what's available at this moment, the Gevachrome 9.03 prints, made by Leo Diner Films of San Francisco, are the best super 8 I have seen, and judging by its performance compared with prints made by its predecessor, 9.02, it has richer color, increased sharpness, finer grain, and less of a tendency toward blocked-up shadow detail.

Now, given these fine print stocks, we need production printing machines designed especially for super 8, not scaled-down 16mm units. Then we'd get real sharpness and picture steadiness.

Ference, Hunt, and McNair, of Eastman Kodak, demonstrated prints made with a very interesting optical printing machine, suitable for low-volume production, at the SMPTE Technical Conference at Los Angeles in October 1977. Their design transfers both image and sound in a single pass through the machine. Since an optical print is made, prestriped base-side print stock can be used. Let me make this clear: Base-striped print stock is available, emulsion-striped stock is not. Emulsion-striped stock must be used for contact prints from camera original so that the proper stripe-perforation orientation is maintained, allowing projector soundheads to contact the track area. Because it is easy to reverse the orientation of an image in an optical printer, the base-striped stock is fine. The exceedingly good prints demonstrated at the SMPTE conference were made on Eastman 7389.

Some people advocate the use of Kodachrome as a camera original since it is so fine grained and sharp. Other people put down the use of this film since it is often difficult to make good prints from it because of contrast buildup. Kodachrome 40 can make very good super 8 prints when used in conjunction with either Gevachrome or

The McNair printer is designed for low-volume, in-house quality super 8 prints. The printer itself is shown on the left, the control unit on the right.

Ektachrome print films. But the major hang-up is that you can't get predictable, dependable results. (I should say that *I* can't get predictable, dependable results.) The usual advice is to avoid contrasty subjects and employ nice flat lighting when exposing Kodachrome meant for printmaking.

But sometimes Kodachrome shot under low-contrast conditions prints well, and other times it doesn't. Very often, high-contrast subjects shot on Kodachrome (for example, people on a sunny beach) will make perfectly good prints, and other times they won't.

The contrast and color of the faster Ektachromes generally come across better in prints, but they are far grainier and less sharp than prints made from Kodachrome originals. However, in many circumstances, these films may produce pleasing prints. (Ektachrome 40, which made the best super 8 prints I've seen, was discontinued in the United States by Kodak because they found sales disappointing. This is a terrible loss for the filmmaker!)

Now the subject of sound. After much trial and error, mostly error, I have settled on Kodak to do most of my print sound striping. Few other labs can apply such a good-quality stripe to the emusion side of contact prints. As you probably know, when contact prints are made from super 8 camera original, the emulsion position changes. While the emulsion of the camera film faces toward the projector lens, contact prints, since they are mirror image, must be oriented with emulsion away from the projector lens. Since this is the case, stripe must be applied to the emulsion side of contact prints if it is to make contact with the soundhead.

There is no emulsion-striped super 8 print material, so all prints must be striped *after* processing. A number of labs offer this service, but from my experience, the stripe is usually of inferior sound quality and often peels off the print. Therefore my advice: Use Kodak for sound striping prints.

Some labs offer sound-transferring services for the super 8 worker, and they can take care of getting the print striped for you along with recording or dubbing the track from your sound master. However, these services are not universally available, and I have come to dub my own sound in my studio. This is a simple procedure, involving no additional equipment if you're already set up to do double-system projection. I have two such setups, a pair of Eumig 824 projectors interlocked by Super8 Sound, and one of the 824s is outfitted with a digital switch which is run in sync with a Super8 Sound recorder. Both methods produce tracks that are far better than anything I have ever heard produced by a 16mm optical track.

That's where it is for me regarding super 8 prints. It takes effort and care to get prints with an adequate image, but if done properly, the prints ought to have superb sound.

The indomitable Rupert Taylor at work.

King of the Basement Stripers

Rupert Taylor ran a successful real estate business in Belmont, California, for many years before he came home for lunch one day and decided it was time to sell the business. He and his wife began to travel, and Taylor started shooting super 8 and adding soundtracks to his films. Though generally pleased with Kodak's poststriping service, a delay of several weeks was involved, and he found their oxide would occasionally fall off the emulsion side of contact prints. Taylor tried various striping services, frequently with disastrous results. So he decided he had to do it himself.

So far, his story parallels that of many people who go into super 8 sound work and wind up with a striping machine. But Taylor went quite a bit farther than anybody I've ever heard of, and now is capable of adding a first-rate stripe, and balance stripe, to either the base or emulsion side of super 8 film.

Rupert Taylor is a tenacious man who, in the effort to get the best possible stripe for his films, learned how to apply a *laminated stripe* of first-rate quality. Now, I must say that I've had my doubts about laminated stripe. Whatever the theoretical advantages may be, practically speaking, this type of stripe can be very troublesome. Laminated stripe is actually a narrow band of recording tape, 25 or 30 thousandths of an inch wide, bonded to film with a solvent. The stripe that Rupert Taylor buys from Agfa has been polished and has its oxide particles aligned by a magnetic field to reduce tape hiss. All to the good, since this is exactly how quality recording tape is made.

Paste, or *liquid stripe,* the alternative method, employs a gooey mixture of binding agent and iron oxide particles spread on film through a nozzle. To keep the stripe uniformly thick, the application must be very even, and iron oxide must be magnetically aligned and the surface of the stripe polished as well. Clearly, paste or liquid application of stripe is an industrial process, one which could not be done with precision by the average home user.

You may be asking, Why even bother with liquid application when we have the laminated process? Although proper thickness, oxide particle alignment, and polishing are built into the laminated process, the stripe in time can tend to pull away from the film. A reduction in signal or fuzzy sound, and sometimes dropout or complete loss of sound, results when the stripe comes up at its edges.

Generally, I tell readers not to bother with do-it-yourself stripe. This is based on my own rather limited experience with a couple of striping machines and reinforcing letters from readers unhappy with their attempts. Moreover, the efforts to apply laminated stripe by some commercial organizations have been disastrous. A caution to be very careful when considering any outfit that claims it can do stripe at very low prices.

Of course, this problem would not exist if Kodak would prestripe their silent super 8 film, that is, their film packed in silent cartridges. As Kodak has it now, the filmmaker who wishes to cut together film shot with a silent camera and film shot with a sound-on-film camera has a terrible problem. The silent film must be striped *before* it is intercut with the single-system sound footage. Polaroid is prestriping all their Polavision cassettes, even though only a silent Polavision camera is available. Also, in Europe you can buy Agfachrome film prestriped in silent cartridges.

When I teach filmmaking, I have my students shoot Ektasound cartridges, even if they are shooting silent and planning to add sound later, to avoid the time lost waiting for striping. Kodak could learn a trick or two from Polaroid or Agfa. Another area of trouble is contact prints made on unstriped stock. For contact print film, the stripe must be applied to the emulsion side of the film, and there is no emulsion-striped print stock. Therefore, super 8 prints must be striped after they are printed and processed, a time-consuming delay involving additional unwarranted expense. In this critical area of sound striping, we continue to face a serious lack in the super 8 system, a deficiency as troublesome to the casual filmmaker as to the serious one.

Several years ago, Rupert Taylor bought a Weberling striper, the industrial model, for his own work. After months of learning the ropes, he succeeded in doing a good job of striping. "I'm still learning," he claims; for even small changes in the procedure can throw everything off.

First, he thoroughly cleans the film with Freon TF, a solvent that has no lubricant. The many products designed for home use, such as Kodak Film Cleaner, have a lubricating action that makes it difficult for stripe to adhere. Film that has already been treated with such a cleaner needs to be cleaned again with Freon TF.

Taylor checks all the film's splices to make sure they're well made and holding up. Then he places the film on his striper and applies the laminated stripe. Taylor uses a jeweler's loupe (magnifying glass) to examine the film to make sure that the application is up to standard. After the stripe has been applied, he treats the film with Tuff Coat to protect and lubricate it.

Rupert also has a $4,000 channeling machine for cutting away emulsion so that stripe may be laminated directly to the base of contact prints. The cutter may also be used to remove faulty stripe. He gets many films from folks who attempted to stripe it themselves, or films with stripe applied by so-called professional labs that is falling off the film. A pass through his cutter, then onto the striper, and the film is as good as new.

What started out as a do-it-yourself project has become a do-it-for-others business. Rupert Taylor has all the striping work he can possibly handle. The world of super 8 is beating a path to his door. I watched Rupert Taylor one day at work, and I can only say that I admire his dedication and expertise. He is a tribute to the cantankerous fortitude that people like to think is at the core of American industry. Without trying, his striping business, which is a labor of love, is in danger of becoming a basement success story. (The address is 500 Middle Road, Belmont, California 94002.)

Another interesting striping service is offered by a friend of Taylor's, Harold F. Olsen (2570 Goodwin Avenue, Redwood City, California 94061). Olsen is an agent for Magnatrack striping, a firm from Sidney, Australia. Based on the 70-foot sample I have, and what experts like Ivan Watson in England have written about it, Magnatrack is an excellent product. It's not a laminate, and reportedly it is not a liquid or paste application. Oddly enough, the process has more in common with offset printing. The stripe is very thin and doesn't require a balance stripe. Whatever lies at the heart of the process, the results, I've heard, produce fine sound. You may want to give it a try.

Short Ends II

Leader

When I'm cutting a film—which seems to be most of the time—I go through plenty of black and white leader. Four feet or so of white leader at both the head and tail of a roll of film protect it from being gobbled up by our marvelously misengineered auto-threading projectors, and a foot of black leader between the start of the picture and the white leader makes for a less jarring transition. In addition, black leader is frequently used between sequences in cut film.

I've gone through many methods of storing the leader I need to have on hand, from hanging up reels of leader on nails driven into walls to putting the stuff in piles of small 50-foot reels. Lately, I have taken to using a method I like very much: I store it on reels meant for ¼-inch magnetic tape, in the cardboard boxes that originally packaged the tape. I make a small slot in the corner of each box so that I can pull off any length of leader I need without opening the box.

At first, I found the reels didn't turn terribly well in the box, so I placed a sheet of waxed paper, the kind used for wrapping food, between the reel and the box. The reels now turn with very little effort, and drawing off the leader I need is a pleasure.

If your leader comes on cores, you don't have to bother putting it on reels. Just leave the core-wound leader intact, and place the waxed paper between it and the bottom of the box.

Leader stored in boxes this way can be conveniently stacked horizontally on shelves.

Cue Cards

I find that repetitive procedures of a certain type drive me up the wall. There are some techniques in filmmaking, especially in post-production, that require an absolutely perfectly executed sequence of actions or that require elaborate logic or reasoning to figure out, for example, whether to move something forward or backward. If you make films, you get the idea by now.

It's torture to have to rethink what is essentially a mechanical procedure. The torturous part is getting the damn thing wrong after thinking the procedure through. The obvious answer is to write down the exact procedure so that you can carry out the action without having to think things through from scratch. I used to put these things in notebooks, but I could never find the proper entry. I've got many notebooks.

Now I write things on index cards. The ones I refer to often are posted where they're needed; others are stored in a file box. I've got cards telling me which way to move the film in my synchronizer when cutting double-system sound after having established proper sync with the Super8 Sound sliding magnetic head, cards telling me the length of fades and dissolves my lab can give me, and cards giving me exposure advice for shooting titles.

Eumig Revisited

After three years of a love affair with Elmo projectors, I've gone back to Eumig machines. It's turned out that they are easier on film than the Elmos, and they accept tape splices better. However, the distinct advantage of the Elmo line for me is the availability of longer focal lengths for projection because of the really good Elmo $f/1.4$, 25 to 50mm zoom lens. When projecting from the rear of a large hall, the standard 15 to 30mm Eumig lens is often just too short and projects an image too large for the screen.

The cure? I use a 16mm projection lens with the appropriate-diameter lens barrel and focal length. The Eumig barrel is about

Eumig 824 two-channel sound projector.

1 3/16 inches in diameter, and many 16mm lenses will fit this standard. In some cases, just a few layers of masking tape or a rolled tube
of paper will shim up the lens to make it fit snugly. I use both an
old RCA 400 and new Kodak Pageant 16mm projector. The 50mm
optics, which are standard on these projectors, work perfectly well
on the Eumig, and many other focal lengths are also available.

The Elmo and Eumig mounts are the same diameter, but lenses are
not interchangeable between the machines because of differences in
the focusing mechanism and castings of adjacent parts. Too bad it
isn't possible to use the Elmo 25 to 50mm lens on the Eumig line. It
might be possible by removing the Elmo lens's focusing pin and filing
or grinding away a body flange next to the Eumig lens mount, but I
haven't tried it, so you're on your own if you're interested in this

conversion. Manufacturers are cursed with a Stone Age mentality vis-à-vis parts interchangeability, which can only lead to making equipment far less useful than it could be.

A Buzzing Squawk Box

I was having trouble with a buzz coming out of my squawk box (amplifier-speaker combination). Although I don't expect high-fidelity sound when cutting with my Super8 Sound motorized editing bench, I also don't expect to be harassed with a loud buzz. I found a cure that is about 90 percent effective in reducing the noise to tolerable levels: I ran a ground wire (a single strand of speaker wire or electronic hook-up wire will do) from the magnetic sound reader to the motor which drives the synchronizer. The wire is run from the bolt which holds the sound reader to the bench to one of the bolts that holds the motor in place.

Save the Slugs

Save short ends of mag film and picture outs for use as slugs when cutting sound track. (Slugs are lengths of film used to take up space, especially useful if you're cutting multiple-channel sound.)

For emotional reasons, I don't use picture for this purpose, but there's no reason why you can't, as long as the base side of the picture slugs are on the same side as the oxide coating of the mag film. I use outs and short ends of mag film with the base (shiny side) reversed so that it's on the side usually used for oxide. This makes it easier to spot sections of slugs when cutting.

The Brightest Screen

In my studio, I have settled on the Kodak Ektalite screen in place of the aluminized lenticular pull-down screen I used in the past. I've used other screens that cost less, but the Ektalite, although it's only

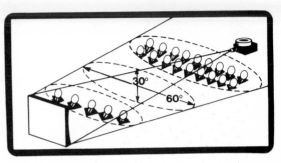

Ektalite screen coverage is about 60 degrees in the horizontal plane, and 30 degrees in the vertical.

40 inches wide and costs $126, is so much brighter, that I've simply fallen in love with it. The screen is rigid, with thin aluminum coating on a cast synthetic material. I mounted it on my ceiling with stove bolts and fence hinges so that I can swing it into place when needed.

Kodak makes only one model, which is 40 inches square. I wish they would make a 54 x 40-inch screen so that the aspect ratio would match the super 8 frame. You can get such a screen from TIW Industries, Inc. (P.O. Box 1546, Rochester, New York 14602) for $342. It's made up of two 40-inch screens spliced together. (I've learned of a similar screen at half the cost made by J. C. Siva, Inc., 1520 N.E. 131st Street, Miami, Florida 33161.)

Although I've ordered one from TIW, I'd prefer the even larger screen made by Advent for their VideoBeam TV projector. Since the TV and super 8 aspect ratio are the same, the Advent screen is a perfect fit. It's Ektalite also, made under license from Kodak. As far as I know, Advent won't supply these 68-inch-wide screens for film projection, but they will supply replacements for these easily marred screens for owners of their VideoBeam projectors.

I used an Advent screen for super 8 projection one summer, and it was so good, that I feel it practically renders all other super 8 projection screens obsolete—unless portability is an important consideration, that is.

All of this is very important because of the fact that super 8 images need more help in terms of reflected screen illumination than images from other movie or slide formats. Why? Super 8 projectors are dimmer than other projectors because of the small size of the format.

There is a definite correlation between image brightness and sharpness, and in this way, the Ektalite screen makes a substantial contribution to overall super 8 quality. Moreover, moderately bright projectors, like the dependable Eumig 807s, do just about as well on these screens as their brighter and more expensive cousins. If only somebody could convince Kodak to make a 54 x 40-inch Ektalite screen, which would give filmmakers nearly double the image area (30 x 40 inches) now available on the present screen.

MXR Stereo Graphic Equalizer

Including an equalizer in the filmmaker's studio setup has become more common these days, in which the equalizer is considered a high-fidelity component. There was a time, not so long ago, when these devices cost many thousands of dollars and could be found only in recording studios. Times have changed, and good-quality instruments are now available for only a few hundred bucks.

An equalizer is a sophisticated base and treble control that can be used to manipulate the audio spectrum. The equalizer most commonly found in the super 8 studios I've visited lately is the BSR graphic stereo equalizer. BSR makes two units—one with many more pots (control knobs) than the other—for increased audio control. Both have two channels (hence the machines are stereo), and both have their control knobs arranged so that they form a visible shape of the audio spectrum as you've set it. The FEW2 has controls for five bands (60, 240, 1,000, 3,500, and 10,000Hz), and the FEW3 has twelve bands (30, 50, 90, 160Hz, and so on).

These are good units, and they let you control the quality of sound as it's being dubbed, say from your original full-coat recording to striped film. You can make a voice sound like it's coming out of a tin can or less than a foot away from the ear, just by fooling with the pots. You can help reduce the camera noise picked up at the time of filming.

One source of noise is especially difficult to deal with when using BSR units, and that's the 60Hz hum produced by line current. Some sound projectors have monstrous magnetic fields, and these can induce hum in even the best shielded magnetic heads (their own or magnetic recorders in their vicinity). The most noticeable sound of the hum comes, perversely, not at 60Hz, but usually at the first harmonic, at 120Hz. You can dip into the frequencies adjacent to 120Hz, but with the price of reducing more important sound than you intended. The BSR units simply don't have bands close enough to the 120Hz frequency. Therefore, I call to your attention the MXR stereo graphic equalizer (BSR, you will recall, uses the term "graphic stereo equalizer"). The MXR, like the FEW3, lists for $200, but it has bands at 31, 62, 125, 250, 500, 1,000, 2,000, 4,000, 8,000, and 16,000Hz, which make it much more suited to the requirements of hum-prone super 8 hardware.

Projection Brightness

Any super 8 projector will be just as bright at 18 fps as it will be at 24 fps. The shutter in the projector cuts off the same portion of available illumination at any frames-per-second rate. You can test this by holding a light meter up to the lens while running your projector without film. The meter will give the same reading with the projector running at either speed.

MXR equalizer.

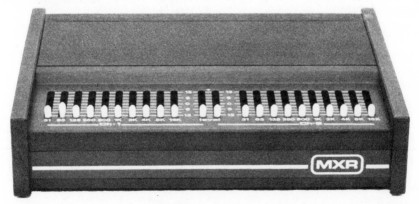

Super 8 projectors have three-bladed shutters that spin rapidly, interrupting the light flow through the lens 54 times per second at 18 fps and 72 times at 24 fps. Generally speaking, 50 interruptions per second are enough to overcome flicker on your viewing screen. If super 8 projectors were set up with two-bladed shutters, as are all machines in commercial theaters which run at 24 fps only, the effective flicker rate would be an adequate 48 at 24 fps, but only an unacceptably low 36 interruptions per second at 18 fps.

Kodak offers an interesting shutter for its AV line of 16mm Pageant projectors: one that's two-bladed for 24-fps operation and three-bladed for 18-fps operation. The increase in illumination at 24 fps compared with 18 fps (two blades obstructing the light path instead of three) is a significant 40 percent! A good idea for super 8 designers to copy. The increase in projected illumination is nothing to blink at.

Brightness depends on the entire optical system of the projector, and that means the lamp and lens combination. In some cases, a more powerful lamp will not put more light on the screen because the projection lens isn't matched to the lamp's capabilities. It's been my observation that increased wattage in super 8 machines, beyond a certain point, goes almost entirely into heat and not illumination. Given two projectors with equal features, I would not automatically opt for a 150-watt over a 100-watt lamp on the basis of rating alone. If you're shopping around for a projector, see if you can get the photo supply store to test a few projectors for you in a darkened room so that you can make a visual comparison. Or again, you might use a light meter.

Section 5

The Shape of Images to Come

Introduction:

Chloe in 1990

My daughter Chloe is seven years old. Someday she may develop a passing interest or, who knows, even a passion for filmmaking. If that happens, I think Chloe, when she is 19 years old—in 1990—will be part of a new filmmaking technology. Most if not all beginners, like Chloe, will come to filmmaking through super 8 in the years to come. Many of them will never venture to any other format, even though they may go on to successful filmmaking careers. Super 8 will have *everything* they need. Future filmmakers in the super 8 format will have the advantages of more technological changes than filmmakers working in any other format. The very newness of super 8 allows for more fresh approaches to the technical problems than 16 and 35mm formats established earlier. I think the clearest, simplest way to demonstrate what will happen is to follow Chloe into the future, through a day a decade or so from now, as she sets out to make a film.

Chloe has decided to make a film of her friends. Some of her shooting will be interviews, and some will show her friends interacting with each other. First, the camera. She could have chosen to shoot the film in 3-D, using a spool-loading double super 8 camera. There's been a great deal of interest in 3-D (three-dimensional) super 8 since the impact of talkies has lessened to some extent. Double

179

super 8, 16mm wide, makes the perfect format for stereo pairs, and special stereo cameras have been developed.

But no, Chloe has decided to go a more conventional route. She will use a sound-on-film machine, a Nizo SS XL, with a $T/1.2$, 5 to 40mm zoom lens. Camera lenses are now more correctly designated by T stops, which are like f stops except more accurate because they take into consideration light losses in the lens system itself. This camera runs absolutely quietly; thus, it features built-in microphones. The one on the front just above the lens is directional, and it records on the usual sound stripe. Its pickup corresponds to the lens's view of the world. A rear mike picks up the filmmaker's voice and records it on the balance stripe. So Chloe's voice will be recorded on a separate sound channel. In the editorial stage, she can decide whether or not to leave in her questions and comments, and, if desired, both channels can be mixed down to one screening channel. The Nizo SS XL accepts 200-foot cartridges and even longer loads.

I think we should take a quick look through Chloe's camera viewfinder. The image can be focused across the entire width of the viewfinder, which is a textured screen. Above, below, and to the sides of the image itself are electronic readouts, similar to the displays used in pocket calculators. You can see information about exposure, depth of field, focal length, distance setting, film capacity, recording level, and battery status. (Sound-on-film super 8 cameras with these features have made 16mm obsolete for TV news gathering. There aren't any news crews any longer—just one person holding a super 8 image-sound recorder.)

Chloe returns home after a morning of shooting, having exposed several cartridges of Kodak SM III Ektachrome (or possibly she'll be using the rapid-processing Polavision system). It's time for processing, so she plugs one of the cartridges into a Supermatic Desktop Processor and passes the few minutes it takes to process the film munching an algae sandwich.

Today, we already have the Supermatic (SM) processor, which costs about $13,000. Entirely automated, it's the size of a large photocopying machine and uses a vastly simplified four-chemical Ektachrome SM process. Chemical costs for processing a 50-foot cartridge, which takes a shade over 13 minutes, is 44 cents. Anybody can work this machine—it's that simple. Only cost and size preclude the SM processor from being in every home. So, it's really not a radical proposition that by the year 1990, we'll have a few models of really compact SM processors within anyone's price range.

Rapid-processing super 8, like the Supermatic or Polavision systems, will revolutionize filmmaking. Filmmakers will be able to see their results almost *instantly*. And although *all* super 8 filmmakers will benefit from the widespread use of rapid-processing machines, think of what it will mean to beginners and film students! Learning will be greatly accelerated and facilitated, with no delay between shooting and screening.

The actual screening or display of super 8 movies 11 years hence is the most ambiguous area I'm tackling. That's because one key component is still not a manufacturable item. Today there are, for example, 200-foot sound-on-film cartridges, the Supermatic processor, and very fast zoom lenses; but where, oh where, is the long-promised wall screen for displaying TV images?

A number of manufacturers, including Sony, Sharp, and G.E., have titillated the press with their research efforts. It seems that every other month there's a magazine article about breakthroughs in wall-screen TV using electroluminescent panels, light-emitting diodes, or liquid crystals, but the wall-screen TV still remains one of the most awaited inventions of the century.

TV display of super 8 movies will have a number of important advantages over present optical projection. A wall screen could be used in any brightly lit indoor environment that now excludes optical projection. In many rooms not designed especially for optical projection, the best seats lie between the projector's beam and the screen. Wall-screen TV would eliminate this problem.

A thin, wall-hung TV screen, used in conjunction with a super 8 videoplayer, might very well turn out to be the only way to look at movies in 1990. Today, we have Kodak's initial effort, the VP-1, which displays super 8 images in conjunction with an ordinary TV set. Tomorrow's videoplayer will be smaller and lighter than the present 45-pound machine, and it will have many features and creative controls, like slow motion and reverse motion, that are lacking in today's VP-1. But most important, it will be used with a screen measured in *meters,* not in inches.

Let's get back to Chloe. After processing the film, she places a spool of processed film into the videoplayer and views her footage on a 2-meter-wide TV screen. After viewing what she's shot several times, she decides to do a rough cut. After cutting out the portions of her footage which don't please her, she screens her film again on the videoplayer, this time getting set to add effects and color corrections.

Since the videoplayer translates the super 8 image into an electronically displayed TV image, any manipulation you can accomplish with the standard controls of a TV set can be added to the film. Cues for fades, color correction, or exposure control are added in the form of digitized pulses, or code, to the balance stripe. These cues are then read by the videoplayer, and it instantaneously makes the appropriate corrections and effects as the film is played back. In addition, slow or speeded-up motion can also be cued, as well as freeze frames. The image could even be flopped right to left or turned from positive to negative.

So, from morning to afternoon, Chloe has shot a film, processed her footage, done a rough cut, and added cues for electronic image control so that she can screen her film with corrections and optical effects on a videoplayer. But this may not be enough for her; she's impatient. Suppose she wants a print the very same afternoon.

The videoplayer uses what is called a *flying spot scanner* to beam a rapidly moving spot of light across a moving super 8 frame. Electronic gizmos monitor that spot of light as it passes through the film image and turn it into the electronic TV signal. Obviously, this is a vastly oversimplified account, but it seems logical that the process could be reversed. Let me explain: If we had a videoplayer hooked up to what I'll call a *videoprinter,* we could transfer super 8 movies electronically from one to the other. In other words, we could make a print which would incorporate all cued effects as well as the sound track. The videoprinter could be loaded with print stock, and a moving spot of light could trace out the image on the moving super 8 film. (Solid-state devices such as LEDs could take the place of the high-voltage flying-spot device.) If that print stock is Ektachrome Supermatic print stock or Polavision phototape, it could be processed very rapidly.

Thus, Chloe not only shoots her film and processes it all in one day, but she also makes a print. Advanced super 8 technology has placed at her disposal a moving-image system that is far more powerful than anything available presently to people working in major motion picture studios or production houses.

As for Chloe's print, she made it for me, her dad, who's on Mars, making the first super 8 feature to be shot there. It's about Martians, who were discovered in 1985. They are little green people, about 2 feet tall. . . .

And that's what you get for listening to a man who likes to make 3-D movies.

Hollywood and the 3-D Cinema in Depth

The basic idea in a stereoscopic movie is to simulate the depth sense we get from having two eyes. An image taken with the right lens must be presented to the right eye, and one taken with the left lens presented to the left eye. While it's a relatively simple matter to do this for individuals looking through stereoscopes, the problem becomes one of formidable complexity for audience presentations. A number of solutions have been attempted, but the best method I know of was first suggested by a British worker, John Anderton, in 1891—namely, the system employing polarized light.

In its modern form, first demonstrated by Land in 1935, sheet polarizers, or filters, are placed over the projection lenses and in spectacles worn by every member of the audience. The axes of polarization of the projector filters and the spectacle filters are aligned to allow one image to pass through, say, the right filter of the spectacles, and so on. In projection, the images are superimposed on the screen, and the filters in the spectacles sort out the appropriate images. In this way, a right image is presented to the right eye and a left image to the left eye.

The first commercial application of the polarized light process was by John Norling, who made films for the 1939 World's Fair in New York. Prior to this, Norling and his associates had been involved in stereoscopic films using the anaglyph, or green-red filter, method in a series of shorts made for MGM in the mid-twenties. Anaglyphs cause eyestrain for most people because of what psychologists term *retinal rivalry*, which is produced by one eye seeing a red image and the other a green image. Moreover, this form of presentation is good only for monochrome, while the polarized light method uses neutral gray filters which allow for full color.

The next major projection of stereo films took place at the Festival of Britain in 1950, under the direction of Spottiswoode. Animated films by MacLaren and the National Film Board of Canada and a live-action film shot with a rig designed by Dudley were shown. While Norling's camera was made up of two 35mm machines mounted side by side, Dudley devised a rig in which both cameras looked into two mirrors set at approximately 45-degree angles. In this way, bulky studio cameras could have an interaxial (distance between the lenses) that approximated human interocular (distance between the eyes—about 65mm).

Then, the Gunzburg brothers, Milton and Julian—a script writer and an eye surgeon—put together a rig made up of two Mitchell cameras after the fashion of Dudley's device. I suppose that they hoped to cash in on the fame of the Festival of Britain and on declining theater attendance blamed on TV. The Gunzburgs finally persuaded independent producer Arch Oboler, of "Lights Out" radio fame, to make a stereoscopic film, *Bwana Devil*, which opened in December of 1952. The rest, as they say, is history. The box office success of *Bwana Devil* had to be accounted for in terms of stereo, and only stereo, since the film had nothing else going for it.

Industry decision makers thought history was repeating itself à la the talkies—and they didn't want to get caught with their pants down, as they had at the end of the silent era. The instantaneous stereo craze created a technological revolution, and once again, the studios were virtually unprepared.

In a six-month period, the studios made about 150 films. In the first six months of 1953, about 50 films were shot in 3-D. Clearly, the conversion to stereo was in progress. One of the reasons usually offered to explain the rapid cooling off of the stereo film (the boom lasted but six months) is that the films were of low quality, and exploitation films at that. Hollywood has always made exploitation films, exploiting stars or fads or gimmicks, and it was to be expected that three-dimensional films would be handled in the worst possible taste. Everything, including the kitchen sink, was hurled out of the screen at the audience.

But even a bleary-eyed examination of the films shows a number of "A" 3-D pictures, including *Kiss Me Kate, Dial M for Murder, Hondo,* and *Miss Sadie Thompson.* These would probably pass muster, although they were projected flat for most bookings because of the public's antipathy for 3-D by the time they were released. But good work was done in "B" films like *Creature from the Black Lagoon* and *House of Wax.* So stereo films were not any worse than flat product! They were made up of the same mix of good and bad that Hollywood has always turned out.

I think the decline and fall of the stereo film can be attributed to problems in the shooting rigs themselves, a lack of stereoscopic photographic experience on the part of otherwise expert technical crews and cinematographers, inadequate quality control on the part of the labs, a system of projection not matched to the abilities of normal human projectionists, and penny-pinching practices on the part of exhibitors. It all adds up to headaches and eyestrain and the demise of 3-D movies in half a year. And the memory still smarts.

Let's consider the shooting rigs themselves. A number of basically similar schemes were developed, usually using two studio cameras mounted on a single lathelike base. Some rigs, like the Gunzburgs' setup, used cameras facing each other shooting into mirrors. Others, like the Fox unit, used one camera shooting the subject's image reflected by a semisilvered mirror and the other shooting through a mirror. The Universal stereo camera used two machines mounted side by side, but one upside down, to obtain the necessary interaxial distance.

Many features—nine including the Warner efforts, if I am not mistaken—were shot with the Naturalvision rig. The minimum interaxial for this unit was 3½ inches. My tests have convinced me that this separation for many focal lengths and subject-to-camera distances produces eyestrain in many viewers because of needlessly expanded screen parallaxes (distance between corresponding left and right image points). Most photography is better accomplished at interaxials that are equal to or less than the nominal 2½ inches given for the human interocular.

Features that I had an opportunity to examine often showed re-centration of optics for closeups or for certain focal lengths, that is, a shift in the position of the optical axes of the taking lenses resulting in spurious screen parallaxes, the most serious being vertical parallaxes, or misalignments of corresponding left and right image points. If one image point is shifted upwards with respect to the other, by even very small values (more than 0.1 degree), the result is an upward sheering of one eye with respect to the other. For most people, this muscular effort causes eyestrain.

There are appreciable differences in planar and stereo photography, and cinematographers in Hollywood in the fifties had little or no experience with stereoscopic work. It's hard to expect anybody to do good work in a medium without some practice, yet this is exactly what the studios seemed to expect of camera people. So several shooting systems were devised to guide the cinematographer. One was published by Spottiswoode and Spottiswoode, another by Hill in the form of a calculator offered by the Motion Picture Research Council, and another in the form of charts and graphs by Levonian. My work with all three has convinced me that the cinematographer would have been better without such help.

The lab's part in all of this is crucial. Timing for the left and right prints must be precisely the same, or dark and light prints will result. Even small differences in left and right image illumination will produce eyestrain. Shifting framelines produced by different printers or other factors will result in print pairs that have vertical parallax.

And a number of serious errors can take place in the projection booth. Matching the focal lengths of both projection lenses must be to within 0.5 percent, and this was not always the case. Both arcs must receive the same amperage or the images will have unmatched illumination. The projectionist must be on guard for shifted framelines to correct for vertical parallax. Although the projectors were electrically interlocked to keep them in sync, the shutters also have to be substantially in phase (opening and closing together), a condition not automatically guaranteed with the equipment employed. The Polaroid Corporation did a study in 1953 of 100 theaters showing stereo films and found that 25 of them had images enough out of sync to be disturbing.

Then, 5 to 10 percent of the population cannot see stereo, and up to another 10 percent have anomalous stereo perception. These figures may seem discouraging, but the fact that there are tone-deaf people hasn't diminished the activity of musicians. The real problem here is that projectionists with anomalous stereo vision might mis-set their equipment to match their own eyes' needs and produce strain in just about everyone else in the theater.

Finally, we come to the exhibitor, who sometimes sought to save money and wound up helping to kill stereo. Sprayed screens cannot do the job that aluminum-surfaced screens can do. Screens painted with pigment simply have much higher ghosting (spurious images) or left and right image cross talk than screens which are made of aluminum metal. Distributors also sought to save pennies on stereo glasses of inferior quality. Nothing could be more foolish than to have every patron looking at the show through second-rate optics, but it was done.

For the past three years I have been shooting and editing stereoscopic films. In that time, I've learned to make stereoscopic films which are very beautiful and which can be looked at without eyestrain. People are thrilled by the experience of looking at good-quality stereoscopic films, and I am thrilled that I am able to make them.

I am using a system with interlocked cameras and projectors that is very similar to the system employed by studios in the fifties, yet I am able to project films that run rings around the efforts of the film industry. This success is attributable to good system design, and to learning how to do stereoscopic photography and projection. I believe that what I have engineered and the method of photography can be applied to larger formats, but my work has been in the convenient and inexpensive super 8 medium. The information in the following pages is designed to give the independent filmmaker what

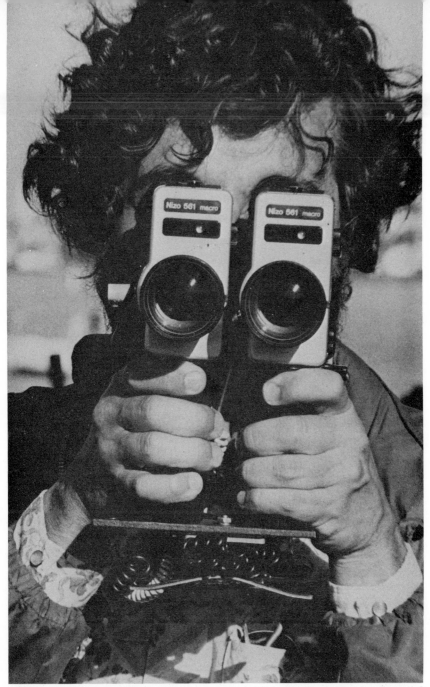

Author holding the Nizo stereo camera (photo by Rod Wyatt, *Super 8 Filmaker*).

she or he needs to know to get started making three-dimensional films. Perhaps smaller is better even when applied to stereoscopic films, for it is a glorious irony that the independent filmmaker now has the means to make excellent-quality stereoscopic films, while the film industry, even with its latest systems, continues to produce nothing but eyestrain.

How to Make Your Own 3-D Movies

Three-dimensional filmmaking in super 8! Sound fantastic? In a way, it is. Forms, shapes, and textures in 3-D are experienced in ways that are closer to our actual perception of the world. And anyone can make their own 3-D films with economical super 8 equipment. I know. I've been doing it for the past two years, and people have described the three-dimensional image I've produced on the screen as "looking out a window."

Depth Perception and 3-D Movies

This is essentially a how-to-do-it chapter, describing tools I've used and techniques I've learned in my research. I believe that any experienced filmmaker who is familiar with double-system sound techniques and possesses good stereoscopic depth perception can master the form. Because of the nature of space limitations, this account must be brief. Anyone interested in a fuller discussion of stereoscopic filmmaking may want to read my book *A Study in Depth: Foundations of the Stereoscopic Cinema* to be published by the University of California Press.

By three-dimensional filmmaking, I'm talking about motion pictures that evoke the unique sensation called *stereopsis*, or "solid seeing," which requires two eyes able to fuse left and right eye images into one integrated depth image. There are other depth cues besides

191

stereopsis, and these were first clearly enunciated by Leonardo da Vinci and other Renaissance painters five centuries ago. They include what psychologists call *interposition, perspective, aerial perspective, relative size, relative brightness,* and *light and shade.*

You know that your friend is between you and the TV set because he's blocking off part of the picture—that's interposition. You've learned to look at the world in terms of receding straight lines which, in the case of railroad tracks, seem to meet at the horizon—perspective. When you see distant hills through a veil of haze, they tend to look farther away—aerial perspective. These *monocular* depth cues (which you do not need two eyes to perceive) comprise the major input we need for judging depth.

While we've enjoyed films with sound and color shown on giant screens and in wide aspect ratios for many years, stereoscopic, or 3-D, cinema has been essentially dormant for the past two decades. Color, sound, giant and widescreen, as well as stereo films were all demonstrated in the first years after the invention of motion pictures, even if public acceptance didn't occur till much later. Essentially there are two reasons why stereo isn't with us today: (1) technical snags and (2) the fact that other depth cues, such as the monocular cues, are conveyed so well by the motion picture medium, that they tend to make the need for stereoscopy less than imperative.

Nevertheless, the sense of depth human beings get from having two eyes is an extremely pleasurable and important sense. Stereopsis has made a basic contribution to human intelligence, and if you want to get down to the nitty-gritty, stereo movies are fun!

Stereopsis wasn't understood to be a separate sense until Sir Charles Wheatstone published his report on his invention of the stereoscope in 1838. Most of us are familiar with the popular modern descendant of Wheatstone's invention, the GAF View Master, which employs seven stereo views mounted on a circular card. The stereoscope presents the left eye with a photo taken by the left lens of a stereo camera and the right eye with a photo taken by the right lens. The mind is able to combine the left and right photos into a single stereoscopic image similar to the way it preceives objects in the real world.

When projecting stereoscopic films on a screen for an audience, the simple solution offered by the stereoscope for getting the appropriate image to the left eye and right eye is of no use. If the images are projected side by side, as they are in a stereoscope, then bulky and costly prismatic "eyeglasses" would be needed. Such devices restrict head movement, which can lead to a great deal of audience discomfort.

On the surface, the requirements for stereoscopic filmmaking sound simple: film left- and right-eye views, and project these so that the left eye sees its view and the right eye, its view. However, there are a number of complex problems that have to be solved first. For one thing, I was faced with a lack of suitable stereoscopic equipment. I decided to tackle the problem by using a double film, mechanical-electronic approach rather than a single film, optical approach. Let me explain. The design and fabrication of an optical system that would record both left and right images on a single film might have cost hundreds of thousands of dollars. But by synchronizing two cameras and two projectors, recording and projecting left and right images on separate films, I was able to spend only a few thousand dollars to obtain the desired results.

It remained to be seen whether or not the super 8 machines at my disposal could do the job. During the first nine months of my study, I vowed that I would call it quits if I could not produce stereoscopic images that were as good as the best images one can see through a stereoscope. I have found that they can, and with them you can create high-quality stereoscopic images that are pleasant to look at for prolonged periods. This is the first time that a stereoscopic motion picture system offering full creative controls has been made available to the small-format filmmaker.

The overall system employs two electronically interlocked Nizo 561 cameras and two mechanically interlocked Eumig sound projectors. You can use a conventional two-sprocket synchronizer editing bench to edit the two films for 3-D projection. The total cost for this system using the Nizo 561s is about $5,000; it should be more than $1,000 less with the Minolta XL-400s.

Although this account is based on the particular Nizo and Eumig machines listed above, I want the reader to understand that many other choices are probably possible. But it is better to discuss procedures in particular terms, since generalizations would lead to overly complicated discussions.

The techniques I use open up stereoscopic films to a vast range of users. This is an ideal system for presenting medical procedures and training films of all kinds, as well as for experimentation by the creative filmmaker, to enumerate only a few areas of use. It's also important to know that all the components in this synergistic system can be disconnected and used individually for conventional filmmaking.

The Stereoprojector and 3-D Projection

It may seem peculiar that I'm going to consider projection before photography, but there are two good reasons for this. In the first place, poor projection has been a major reason why stereoscopic filmmaking hasn't gained an accepted place in the technology of cinema. Second, the conditions of projection actually determine the technique of photography. Without clearly understanding the projection system, it is impossible to do good stereoscopic photography.

The projectors used in the system are made in the Eumig factory. Since they make most of the Bolex sound machines, these can also be employed. As far as the Eumig line itself is concerned, you'll achieve adequate illumination for a 1-meter-wide image with the Eumig 807 projector. But you'll probably need models 810, 820, 822, or 824 for larger screens. (The accurate frame counters on the 820 series are particularly useful for establishing synchronization during the editorial phase of production.)

The machines run in sync using a kit by Super8 Sound (95 Harvey St., Cambridge, Massachusetts 12140), originally devised for image-sound interlock projection (running a film in one projector in sync with a full-coat magnetic soundtrack in the other). I have made a stereoscopic version of this interlock, based on my adaptation of their original design. One machine sits above the other, resting on a flat wooden platform that bolts to the lower projector's carrying handle.

In addition to the platform, the kit includes timing gears, which

Double band stereo projector (front view) is my original unit, using a pair of Eumig 807s. The sheet polarizers, in slide holders, are shown mounted in front of the lenses. I currently employ a pair of brighter Eumig 824s with accurate frame counters which simplify syncing up footage.

Double band stereo projector (rear view) is shown with timing belt running from top to bottom inching knobs that have been replaced by timing gears.

replace the Eumig's original inching knobs, and a timing belt that couples the projectors together. One of the gears is fitted with a simple clutch device for decoupling the projectors for establishing sync or for rewind.

Don't be put off by the fact that one projector is higher than the other. It may seem peculiar, since both our eyes and the lenses of the stereo camera are in horizontal alignment. But this projection arrangement successfully produces overlapping images that coincide well within necessary geometric tolerances. Having one projector above the other simply permits easy access to the controls of both machines.

During projection, the interlocked Eumig machines may be stopped or run in reverse without losing sync. The machines may also be used to mix down two sound channels to one track when running in sync with a magnetic film (full-coat) recorder. These projectors can also serve as dual-screen projectors, keeping left and right images in sync on adjacent screens for multimedia presentations. They are also perfect for changeover operation, allowing uninterrupted screenings of any length. And while in the stereoscopic mode, the projectors can provide two-channel sound, similar to stereophonic sound.

After you've set up the double-band stereo projector, the next important step is to set up the screen properly. A Kodak Ektalite screen, either in its original 40 x 40-inch form or modified 40 x 54-inch model fabricated by TIW (P.O. Box 594, Rochester, New York 14602), must be used, as you will see. Light is reflected from this screen in a highly directional manner, and poor adjustment for a given screening space will result in a dim image. It is possible to adjust the screen-projector relationship to maximize the light from both projectors. Alignment instructions come packed with the screen.

These stereo glasses—cardboard models supplied by Marks—have very good optical properties.

Next, you'll have to adjust the projectors' zoom lenses so that they produce images of exactly the same size. Without film in the machines, project the beams on the screen and zoom the lenses so that the images are exactly the same size. You'll also need to adjust the elevation feet so that the images perfectly coincide. You then use an SMPTE registration test film (available from the Society of Motion Picture and Television Engineers, 862 Scarsdale Avenue, Scarsdale, New York 10583; you purchase one print for about $20, and cut it in half for left and right projectors) to help fine tune this first approximation.

Project the SMPTE films in both machines to perfect focus. You want to wind up with two images projected on top of each other and aligned as impeccably as possible. Not only should the images be exactly the same size, but they should also have their vertical and horizontal edges parallel. When this is done, they will be in what I call the *crossed lens axes* (CLA) mode. In other words, the optical axes of the lenses must perfectly cross at the surface of the screen to achieve CLA.

On the test films, you'll notice the line marked M=.050. This is one key to setting up the lenses. Use the frameline control of one of the projectors to raise one of the M=.050 lines so that it is right above the other for easy comparison. Are the lines marked by the arrows the same length? If not, adjust one of the zoom lenses till they are. Are the lines parallel? If not, you can tilt the top projection platform by adjusting the elevation of the leg holding it up until the

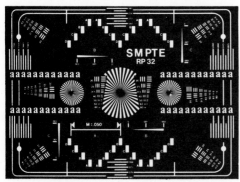

SMPTE registration test film is used for aligning projectors to the crossed lens axes mode.

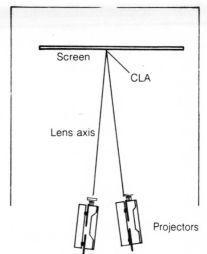

Crossed lens axes setup for projection.

lines are parallel. (You may have to add paper shims under the projector legs.) Now adjust the frameline controls so that the M=.050 lines coincide, or more properly, so that the center circular test patterns coincide. You do this by laterally shifting or slightly rotating the top projector until the CLA condition is achieved.

The resulting twin image should look as if it is being projected by one machine. Only at the extreme corners of the screen should you be able to find any doubling of the images indicating that two projectors are at work. Make sure the image bleeds onto the black border of the screen an inch or two to provide crisp edges. Otherwise, stereoscopic projection can be quite annoying.

After the projectors are aligned in the CLA mode, properly tension the timing belt as explained in the manual that comes packed with the double-band stereo kit.

The next step is to place sheet polarizers over the projection lenses. Their holders should be marked LEFT and RIGHT, respectively, and must be placed on the appropriate machine (the left is the higher projector). The filters are neutral in color, making it possible to screen films in color. I stress this because I'm always asked why the filters aren't green and red. That's another system, which is quite obsolete in the present context.

The purpose of the projector polarizers and viewer polarizers is to transmit the right image to the right eye and the left image to the left eye. This is the same thing that is accomplished in an ordinary stereoscope, like the View Master device. The polarizing material for each eye of the glasses is set at an angle (45 and 135 degrees, respectively) that matches the projector polarizers and, thus, selects the appropriate right or left image for the eye.

Sheet polarizers for projector filters and polarizing glasses are available from Technical Polarizer Division, Polaroid Corporation (20 Ames Street, Cambridge, Massachusetts 02139) and Marks Polarized Corporation (153-16 10th Avenue, Whitestone, New York 11357). They both make good products of comparable quality and price.

The screen is a crucial part of the projection optical system. The light reflected by the screen must preserve the polarization characteristics determined for it by the sheet polarizers mounted on the projector lenses. If the screen depolarizes the incident light, then the image meant for the left eye only, for example, will pass through the right filter of the stereo glasses, creating a ghost image. Many screen surfaces will result in strong ghost image, or cross talk. However, a screen with an aluminum surface, like the Kodak Ektalite, produces essentially no cross talk.

The type of screen you use is also important because the sheet polarizers lose not quite three-quarters of each projector's starting illumination. We need to boost the available illumination by three or four times to get back to where we would have been without polarizers. The Ektalite has very high gain, some three or four times the gain of a beaded or lenticular screen, and the result is a good, bright image without ghosting.

Screening the 3-D Film

Now let's turn our attention to the actual screening of a stereo film. Let's suppose you have a completed film or a work in progress with appropriate sync marks. Punched-hole sync marks are best, and may be observed by looking directly through each lens with the projector plugged in but with the lamps off. The lamps receive a low-voltage standby current in the OFF position—enough light to observe the sync marks. With the interlock declutched, each band may be jockeyed into position by running the motor or by hand inching. Once you can observe both sync marks, clutch the projectors together. It's possible to have the shutters of these machines running to within 10 degrees of each other out of the 360-degree intermittent cycle of pull-down and projection by carefully adjusting the timing belt and by observing the shutters of both projectors. My experiments show that accuracy to 100 degrees is all that's actually needed for projection.

When threading up your films, make sure that the left-hand film is on the left machine, and so on, to prevent "pseudoscopic," or false, images that can be disturbing to the eye. I use a system of one hole punched at the very head of the right film and two at the head of the left to keep things straight.

Above, I've assumed that your footage has been synced, but it may not be when it returns from processing. The cameras do not start and stop at the same instant, and there may be a few frames difference between left and right bands. If you use a clapboard or slate during shooting, simply put the left and right bands on the Super8 Sound motorized editing bench, and, by observing the closed position of the clapper in the viewer, adjust the films until sync is achieved.

It's also possible to find sync with the projectors if shots haven't been slated during shooting, which may be the most convenient way to go while shooting on the run. In this case, you declutch the projectors and adjust by hand, cranking one machine clockwise or counterclockwise until sync is established. Having the lamps in the OFF, or STANDBY, setting as before may provide enough illumination for the Ektalite screen for you to see when the pairs of stereo frames are in sync. To make sure they are, clutch the machines together and project in the usual way.

After sync has been established, you can use a yellow grease pencil to make a mark on the frames at the bar on top of the autothreading entrance. A projector like the 824 (with its accurate frame counter) can simplify the process, since you can tally start marks by making a two-column list labeled "right" and "left." After syncing an entire pair of rolls, place them in the editing bench, and the yellow grease-pencil marks or notations serve as a guide for syncing the bands.

When you're ready to project, both films have to be focused perfectly. This can be done by running both projectors, turning off one lamp to focus the other lens. You can also set focus with the "projectionist's helper," a special double pair of stereo glasses. These are made by cutting a pair of cardboard viewers in half and then taping the halves to either end of another pair. By looking through the left end, only the left image is seen; through the right end, only the right image is seen. Looking through the middle will give you the stereoscopic image.

It is also exceedingly important to set the frameline controls accurately. If they are not aligned, they will cause discomfort and eyestrain, since one eye is forced to turn upwards with respect to the other. Corresponding left and right image elements must be placed at the same horizontal level. Once the frameline controls have been adjusted, you shouldn't have to readjust them often. Make sure you align the images for the central portion of the picture. Whatever the perceptual mechanism involved, the comparison

Projectionist's helper. Through the left pair you can see the left image; the right pair gives you the right image; and from the center position you see a stereo image.

of these superimposed images can be tricky, so care must be taken with this adjustment. It may take a couple of shots to tweak the controls just so.

Finally, I ought to mention that Bonum reels and cans, which clip together, are perfectly suited to the needs of the medium. These are imported by Eumig, and are available from most super 8 retailers. The cans have four circular locking devices, similar to clothing snaps. Any number of same-size cans can be clipped together to store reels. For example, three can be clipped together to hold left and right image reels and a reel of magnetic sound.

You now have the basic information needed to get started with stereoscopic projection. Of course, you have nothing to project until you shoot some stereoscopic footage.

The Stereo Camera and Photography

The Nizo 561 cameras turn out to be a very good choice for 3-D filming because the machines can be easily crystal controlled. That is, their filming speeds may be regulated so that the cameras run in sync with each other. This is done with electronics similar to those used in digital watches. The Nizos are also small enough to be mounted close together for 3-D shooting. They are rear loading, which simplifies changing film once the cameras are mounted side by side. And they've got one more thing going for them—they're darn good cameras. (Sad to say, they are difficult to obtain at the present time, despite the fact that they remain in production.)

The Nizo cameras are modified so that they can be controlled with Super8 Sound crystal units, originally designed for running camera and recorder in sync for double-system sound recording. The crystals allow the cameras to be used individually, or as part of the stereoscopic ensemble, to film lip-sync sound without cables. The adapted Nizo cameras will operate only at 24 fps when they are set up with crystal controls for 3-D shooting.

You'll remember that I've also taken advantage of existing sync-sound systems for projection. All the components of this stereo-scopic filmmaking system may be detached and used separately for conventional, or "2-D," silent or sound filmmaking.

Nizo stereo camera mounted on handheld base.

In my initial experiments with a pair of crystal-controlled Beaulieu 4008 cameras, I learned that simply synchronizing cameras isn't good enough for stereoscopic filmmaking. The shutters must also be in phase; they must open and close at precisely the same instant. In other words, cameras running independently, each crystal controlled, will run in sync, but there is no guarantee that the shutters are opening and closing simultaneously. The result of this out-of-phase stereoscopic filming is a peculiar rippling, or jellylike effect, accompanying moving objects like people's limbs.

To solve this, I reasoned that both cameras would have to be

Minolta stereo camera mounted on Edmund rack-and-pinion tripod base.

controlled by the same crystal source, and Jon Rosenfeld, research director of Super8 Sound, designed a special modification of two Super8 Sound crystal units to accomplish this. The actual work of modification was carried out by Bob White, an expert in motion picture synchronization systems who, in effect, lobotomized one of the crystals in one of the control units and plugged it into the other unit. The control units maintain their original function, but by plugging one into the other, they offer stereoscopic camera sync, too.

For 3-D filmmaking, the two cameras must be mounted on a base. The handheld design of the Nizo camera is fairly compact and also works well for tripod operation. The base is made of aluminum stock 5mm thick, 50mm wide, and 140mm long.

In the handheld mode, both shutter buttons are released or squeezed with both hands simultaneously. For tripod operation, you may find it more convenient to start the cameras with cable releases or remote control units. The people at Edmund Scientific (555 Edscorp Building, Barrington, New Jersey 08007) were kind enough to adapt a rack-and-pinion unit originally intended for use as an optical bench for a tripod base. This superb piece of equipment allows you to vary the interaxial distance (between the lenses) from 50mm to 200mm.

Matched pairs of cameras that are optically aligned and have calibrated instrumentation must be used. You can set the aperture, focusing control, and focal lengths of these matched cameras by the scales engraved on the lens mounts or, visibly, by looking through the viewfinder. The density, image size, and focus must be within tolerance for the left and right cameras. It's also critically important that the camera axes are aligned in the same horizontal plane. They must be perfectly level with each other, or your photography will project with vertical parallax, in which left and right image points are out of alignment. If vertical parallax exceeds more than 0.1 degree, observers will feel discomfort, since one eye will be forced to turn upwards with respect to the other. This isn't necessarily harmful, but it never occurs in real life, and using muscles this way will be interpreted as strain. Vertical parallax is not interpreted as depth information; only horizontal parallax or the displacement of corresponding left and right image points are so interpreted.

Calibration or matching of the cameras may be carried out in several ways. The cameras could be turned into projectors by inserting a cartridge fitted with a lamp and reticule, or target, in the gate. In this way focal length, focus, lens transmission, and alignment of the lenses' axes in the horizontal plane may be instantly observed and measured.

Another alternative would be to do photographic tests of a target. This would mean analyzing the tests upon projection and keeping careful records.

It's also possible to set the cameras' shutters so that they remain open; the cameras can be left running for this, and you can view through the lenses, straight through the film chamber, no cartridge in place. Looking at a test target with the aid of a magnifying glass can help you calibrate the camera lenses.

Stereoscopic Depth Perception

The mind is able to turn the two flat images projected by the eyes' lenses on each retina into a three-dimensional image of the world. This is called *fusion*. When you look at any particular object, you see it singly, not as a double image. For example, hold a finger in front of your eyes and look at it. You see one finger, but the objects behind your finger will actually appear to be double until you change focus and look at them. Once your eyes converge on some new point in space, you see it as a single image. The rotation of your eyes by their muscles to bring about fusion is called *convergence*. In our case, once the eyes converge on a point behind the finger, it's the finger that's seen double.

If you were to examine the images on the left and right retinas, you'd see that the object on which the eyes have converged is projected on the central portion of each retina. Generally you're not aware of it, but the images projected by your eyes' lenses on other portions of the retina are perceived as double images. That's what I tried to illustrate with the finger example, which was actually first suggested, in a somewhat different form, in the second century by the physician Galen in *On the Use of the Parts of the Human Body*. It's possible to pass an entire lifetime never realizing that most of what you're looking at is being seen as a double image.

The difference between corresponding points of the left and right retinal images, produced by the horizontal displacement of your eyes, is called *disparity*. The analogous quantity for the stereoscopic camera is called *parallax*. Parallax may be measured simply as the distance between two points on the film, or as finally projected on the screen. The mind turns the disparity seen in the visual world, or in a stereoscopic projection of a film, into a sense of three-dimensional depth, or stereopsis.

How 3-D Films Have Depth

I'm going to jump quickly from the eye to the 3-D projector and screen. If a stereoscopic projection produces right and left object points that exactly coincide (*zero parallax*) on the screen, the object will appear to be in the plane of the screen. If the right and left points have what we call *positive screen parallax,* then the object will appear to be deep in the screen, or in what I call *screen space.* If the object points are crossed for *negative screen parallax,* the object will then appear to be in what I call *theater space,* or in front of the screen. When we view objects in these three areas of screen parallax, we get a sense of three-dimensional space.

There is one additional screen parallax condition, namely that of *divergence,* in which our eyes must move outwards in order for fusion of left and right image points to take place. The eyes don't usually have to diverge, so some discomfort may be experienced. Divergent screen parallax is important because it's very difficult to do stereoscopic photography and projection without it. As the right and left lenses of the stereo camera converge, which is necessary for filming objects close to the camera, right and left points of distant objects will spread apart. When such a shot is projected, these corresponding points of background objects may be farther apart than the distance between your eyes. If this is the case, your eyes must diverge in order for fusion to take place.

A small amount of divergence is allowed in my system. The great majority of people have no trouble fusing such images and experience no discomfort while viewing stereo movies shot this way. The depth-range table given at the end of this section was calculated on the basis of one degree total divergence (combined for both left and right eyes), assuming that the closest seats will be no nearer than a distance equal to twice the screen width. The farther you sit from the screen, the less the divergence.

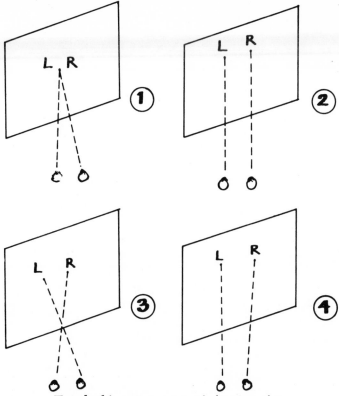

Eyes looking at stereoscopic image points.

1. Left and right image points coincide (zero parallax). Point will appear to be in the plane of the screen.
2. Image points are the same distance apart as the eyes, and lines drawn from each eye to the point it sees do not cross. Image point will appear to be some great distance in screen space. This is an example of positive parallax.
3. Image points are the same distance apart as the eyes, but lines drawn from each eye to the point it sees will cross. This is defined as negative screen parallax. Image point will appear to be halfway between observer and screen, or in what I call "theater space."
4. Similar to positive parallax, but image points are actually farther apart than distance between eyes, leading to divergence. In all other cases, eyes must angle inward or converge, while here they angle outward slightly or diverge. Such object points will appear to be at some great distance from the observer.

Stereo Cinematography

We are using a crossed lens axes (CLA) system for projection. If you understand this, you should be able to see how it applies to 3-D shooting with the stereo camera. An object which is filmed with the lens axes converged on it during photography will appear to be in the plane of the screen when projected. Objects behind the point or plane of convergence will appear in screen space, and objects in front of the plane of convergence will appear in theater space, or in front of the screen.

You should do most of your 3-D filming with objects at the plane of the screen or in screen space. If objects are to be brought forward from screen into theater space, be careful not to cut the object off by the screen edges. This is especially important for the vertical edges of the frame. Many viewers will feel discomfort if objects with parallax—indicating they are in front of the screen—are cut off by the edges of the screen, which projectionists call the *surround.*

When filming stereoscopic motion pictures, the filmmaker can completely control the location of objects in the subsequent 3-D projection by properly covering the lens axes. The camera view-finders themselves are used for setting convergence. If, for example, you had a vertical line inscribed in the center of each viewfinder, you could align these vertical lines to coincide on an object during photography. The lens axes of the cameras would then cross on that object, and upon projection, the object would appear to be in the plane of the screen. (This method was first proposed by Alfred Smee in 1854.)

Most cameras don't have a convenient vertical line, but the rangefinder circles of the calibrated Nizo cameras can be used to set convergence in the same way. The point of intersection of the horizontal line with the left or right portion of the rangefinder circle will serve as a reference point.

Make sure you set convergence at the extreme telephoto position to ensure the greatest accuracy. Since you'll be dealing with the setting of angles of from 0.2 to 4 degrees, you need all the accu-

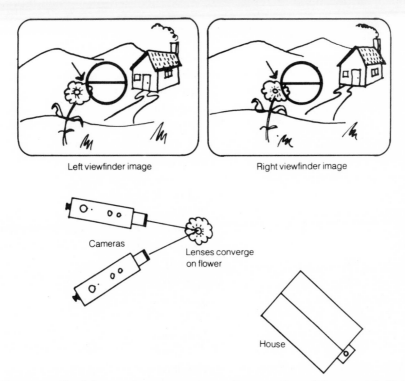

Left viewfinder image   Right viewfinder image

Cameras

Lenses converge
on flower

House

**Target method for setting convergence. Intersection of horizontal divid-
ing line of split-image viewfinder with circle provides a point for alignment. Both finders are aligned on the flower, which will appear in the
plane of screen while the house will appear in background.**

racy you can get. Do your first photography on a tripod. Setting
convergence with a handheld rig can be done, and that's the way
I've used the cameras most of the time, but it's difficult. You ought
to get lots of practice with tripod work before you attempt it.

All photography you do with this CLA system must have some
convergence, including shots of very distant subjects. Some people
assume that distant-object shooting would call for the lens axes
to be parallel. If the cameras were set up this way, given CLA
projection, distant-object points would have zero parallax and

appear in the plane of the screen. (I've included recommendations for setting convergence for shots of distant subjects in a depth-range table, which is discussed later.)

For handheld work, I've found that it's convenient to leave the axis of one camera perpendicular to the baseline (the line between the centers of both tripod sockets) and set convergence by rotating the other camera. This allows for simple and more rapid setting of convergence. The camera which is fixed in position incorporates a shim between it and the base, used to align the lenses' axes to the horizontal plane, thus avoiding vertical parallax.

Another new camera variable for stereoscopic filmmaking is setting the *interaxial distance,* or the distance between the lenses. This setting correlates with the distance between the human eyes, which is called the *interocular distance.* (The average interocular distance is about 65mm for males and 63mm for females.) Generally speaking, much stereo photography can be successfully accomplished with interaxial distances that fairly closely match the interocular.

The setting of convergence and interaxial has been the subject of intense debate since the middle of the nineteenth century, when Sir David Brewster and Sir Charles Wheatstone, two usually respectable physicists, clashed, stopping a hair short of name-calling. (Actually it was Brewster who behaved peevishly.) The modern literature on the subject reflects markedly different points of view on how to film stereo successfully. The system of photography I'm describing was arrived at by my actually doing stereoscopic filmmaking, something very few people have had the privilege of doing with a system capable of varying the creative controls of convergence and interaxial.

Let's return to the subject of setting the interaxial. Closeups can often profit from reduced interaxials (camera lenses set close together). Having the lenses set close to each other is also good for photography with wide-angle or short focal length lenses (say, those under 10mm) when shooting objects in the medium-close range (1 to 5 meters away). Photography of rather distant objects, of, say, 100 meters away, might well be done with extended interaxials, where the camera lenses are set far apart.

The Nizo cameras cannot have their interaxial reduced to less than the average interocular, or about 66mm. Despite this, I used the cameras extensively for closeup work of flowering cacti by making sure that the background is fairly close (100 to 500mm) to the object at the plane of convergence. Because of the extreme convergence needed for closeups, background points tend to diverge rather quickly, which can lead to a great deal of viewer discomfort. By using a textureless, even background, like cardboard, there are no background points to fuse, and the depth range is effectively extended.

An alternative technique I've employed with a camera on the Edmund rack-and-pinion base is to photograph both left and right images with one camera. This can reduce the interaxial distance for extreme closeups of subjects which aren't moving. First, the left shot is taken, then the same camera is racked through the appropriate distance for the right shot. For example, closeups to show the relief of a coin or the textures of the surface of an oil painting might require interaxials of 5 to 20mm. Since you'll be projecting a tremendously magnified image of the object—in a way it is normally never seen—a little bit of depth exaggeration can help to produce visually stunning effects.

Distant-object shots also benefit from an extended interaxial. Because they are electronically interlocked, you can set the cameras on an exceedingly large base, even hundreds of meters apart, provided there is enough connecting cable and a satisfactory method for aligning the cameras. This kind of photography is called *hyperstereoscopy*, and the following relationship has been given for determining a suitable base $t = D/50$, where t is the interaxial and D is the distance from the camera to the object to be filmed. For example, I live on top of a hill, and I'm looking at some tankers in the bay at this very moment. If I wanted to film the tankers, which are about a kilometer away, I'd need to use a base of 1/50 kilometer, or 20 meters. Most photography, however, can be carried out by setting the cameras in the neighborhood of the 65mm interocular distance. Hyperstereoscopy is admittedly a special branch of the art.

Finally, we come to the innovation I feel a great deal of pride in presenting—the *depth-range table*. It seems an obvious idea, but

214   Lipton on Filmmaking

nothing like it exists. I cannot in this space explain how I calculated the table, but let me say that it assumes an interaxial of 67mm (the interaxial distance of my rig), a screen size of 1.4 meters, and a spectator no closer than about 2.5 meters from the screen. It will work perfectly well for smaller screens with people sitting correspondingly closer, and it will give reasonably accurate values for interaxials to within about 5 percent of 67mm.

DISTANCE TO PLANE OF CONVERGENCE
(Meters)

Focal Length		1.0	1.1	1.2	1.5	1.7	2	2.5	3	4	6	Distant Shots
7mm	near	.70	.75	.79	.91	.99	1.08	1.21	1.32	1.48	1.69	
	far	6.80	17.79	∞	∞	∞	∞	∞	∞	∞	∞	2.35
9mm	near	.75	.81	.86	1.00	1.09	1.20	1.37	1.50	1.72	2.01	
	far	2.97	4.07	5.88	3.02	∞	∞	∞	∞	∞	∞	3.02
12mm	near	.80	.86	.92	1.09	1.19	1.34	1.54	1.72	2.00	2.41	
	far	1.99	2.43	2.98	5.91	11.02	4.02	∞	∞	∞	∞	4.02
15mm	near	.83	.90	.97	1.16	1.27	1.43	1.67	1.88	2.23	2.73	
	far	1.66	1.96	2.30	3.72	5.26	9.80	5.03	∞	∞	∞	5.03
20mm	near	.87	.94	1.02	1.23	1.36	1.54	1.82	2.07	2.50	3.17	
	far	1.43	1.64	1.87	2.72	3.45	4.96	9.85	28.71	∞	∞	6.70
28mm	near	.90	.98	1.06	1.29	1.44	1.65	1.97	2.27	2.80	3.66	
	far	1.27	1.44	1.61	2.21	2.67	3.49	5.35	8.33	27.19	∞	9.38

TABLE OF NEAR AND FAR PLANE LIMITS
Interaxial = 67mm

Depth range table figured for interaxial of 66mm. Suppose you are shooting with lens set at 15mm, and your plane of convergence is 1 meter. Then this chart tells you that objects further than 1.7 meters will have excessive divergence.

Here's how you might use the table: Suppose you want to do a shot of a person 1.5 meters in front of your cameras, and you want to use the 15mm focal length. How far can the background be placed from the person, assuming you've set the cameras so that the person is in the plane of convergence? The top line of the table gives the distance from the camera to the point or plane of convergence, in our case 1.5 meters. Checking the vertical column which lists camera focal lengths, under the heading *Far*, 15mm crosses 1.5 at the distance 3.72 meters. That means you ought not to allow the background to be more than 3.72 meters from the camera.

If the shot won't work as you've first planned it, try moving the subject closer to the background or using a shorter focal length.

Objects can also be placed in front of the plane of convergence, so that they'll appear to be in front of the projection screen, by placing them no closer than the entry listed under *Near*. For our case this is 1.16 meters. Objects placed at this distance from the camera will appear to be halfway between the screen and audience, in theater space. If you film objects closer than this, you will probably strain many eyes, especially those of people sitting near the screen. And please remember my cautionary words about objects projected so that they appear in front of the screen: Don't cut off these objects by the screen surround.

If you want to film a far-off landscape, use the *Distant Shots* column on the depth-range table. Suppose you want to shoot a vista with the 7mm setting. The cameras must be set so that they have a plane of convergence 2.35 meters away. Use some target— a friend, for example—at the proper distance to set the convergence, employing the camera rangefinder circles as described (Smee's method). Once the cameras have been set, remove the target and take the shot.

Corresponding left and right image points photographed using the entries in the *Distance Shots* column will have a screen parallax equal to the interocular distance. In other words, no divergence is allowed in this case. I remind the reader that divergence is assumed for the *Far* entries, which is acceptable since the corresponding background points are less important than the foreground.

It seems peculiar as I conclude a discussion on what I've learned in three years of concentrated effort, that I haven't said a great deal about how much I love stereoscopic filmmaking. Well I do, and so will many of you. My system has been enthusiastically received wherever I've shown it, from the Toronto Super 8 Film Festival to the International Super 8 Film Festival in Caracas, and many points in between.

No words can explain how lovely, rich, and strong this medium is. I feel I've overcome the difficulties in former systems which employ sheet polarizers for image selection. I have had the privilege of showing stereo images to many people who had been turned off to the medium by systems that produced eyestrain and headaches—rather than beautiful images. While the industry was unable to properly shoot and project three-dimensional movies, you can.

Index

[*Italic* page numbers indicate illustrations.]

Lenny Lipton was born May 18, 1940 in Brooklyn, New York. He was educated in the New York City public schools and attended Cornell University where he received his B.A. in Physics in 1962.

At the age of nineteen he composed the lyrics to "Puff, The Magic Dragon." Since then, he has become a prolific expert in the field of filmmaking. He is the author of the critically acclaimed *Independent Filmmaking* and of *The Super 8 Book.*

Presently he is researching stereoscopic filmmaking, and he is the first independent filmmaker to produce live-action subjects in the three-dimensional medium.